MW01626116
COLLECTOR'S EDITION
Entertainment
WEEKLY
THE
THE ULTIMATE GUIDE TO
AVENGERS

Josh Brolin's powerful Thanos prepares to smash-and-grab his way to a complete Infinity Gauntlet.

Contents

MARVEL'S MIDAS TOUCH

From *Iron Man* to *Black Panther,* Marvel Studios' unparalleled run of critically acclaimed megahits has reshaped Hollywood—transforming superhero tales into pop-culture gold. **BY SEAN SMITH**

IT'S HARD TO IMAGINE NOW, BUT A DECADE ago no one had ever heard of a "cinematic universe." Robert Downey Jr.'s highest-grossing film was the 1986 Rodney Dangerfield comedy *Back to School,* and no movie he'd ever starred in had cracked $100 million. The only superhero TV show was *Smallville.* Comic-Con was not a thing—at least the way it is now. And nobody, outside of hardcore comic-book fans, could identify Ant-Man or the Guardians of the Galaxy or—Odin, help us—find Asgard on a map.

Spider-Man 3 had managed to become the highest-grossing film of 2007, just ahead of *Shrek the Third,* but its domestic box office had dropped more than $60 million from the first installment, and the franchise was fading. The Top 10 for the year teamed with *Transformers* and pirates, but not a single other superhero film cracked the Top 15.

So to say that Marvel Studios has redefined global pop culture skirts the edge of understatement. In the past 10 years, starting with *Iron Man*'s expectation-shattering $585 million success in May 2008, Marvel Studios, led by president and superproducer Kevin Feige, has cranked out a staggering 16 films that have raked in more than $13 billion worldwide. That alone would be impressive. But in so doing, Marvel also revolutionized Hollywood in ways large and small. Geek culture is central to American culture and

In 2018 *Black Panther* soared to new box office heights. From left: Nakia (Lupita Nyong'o), T'Challa (Chadwick Boseman) and Okoye (Danai Gurira).

In 2012 *The Avengers* assembled the team for the first time. From left: Black Widow (Scarlett Johansson), Thor (Chris Hemsworth), Captain America (Chris Evans), Hawkeye (Jeremy Renner), the Hulk (Mark Ruffalo) and Iron Man (Robert Downey Jr.).

Tony Stark launched Marvel's modern era in 2008 with the breakout hit *Iron Man*.

has become the primary—and perhaps only—vehicle for turning (or re-turning) actors into bankable superstars. How did that happen?

Before *Iron Man,* Marvel Films, as it was then called, didn't make movies. Instead it just licensed its characters to producers and studios who made them. This system worked with Sony's *Spider-Man* and FOX's *X-Men* movies, but overall the results were either uneven (*Daredevil, Blade,* two *Fantastic Four* movies) or disastrous (*Elektra*). The conventional wisdom was that Marvel's arsenal of characters simply wasn't high-profile enough to compete with DC titans Batman and Superman.

But Feige had a vision—if Marvel could become its own studio and make the films themselves, these characters could be woven into one massive interconnected narrative. Marvel's first horse out of the gate was *Iron Man,* and the casting of Downey proved key. At the time, he had overcome years of addiction and a prison term. Hollywood and moviegoers rooted for him to make a comeback. It was a huge gamble for everyone involved, but it paid off in large part because Feige believed then, and now, that the success of these films depended on being faithful to the comic-book characters and stories. Build it for the fanboys and girls, and the rest of the culture would follow.

Today many major talents from Robert Redford to Angela Bassett, Tilda Swinton to Cate Blanchett have appeared in Marvel movies. The studio has made A-listers of all three Chrises, Mark Ruffalo and many more—including newly minted box office king Chadwick Boseman, whose *Black Panther* has broken just about every box office record there is. The Marvel Cinematic Universe structure has been copied by both Lucasfilm's Star Wars films and, in its own way, by Warner's DC films. Now, as the first chapter of the Avengers movies edges toward a close with *Infinity War* and 2019's finale, Marvel prepares for its next exciting phase.

Worlds await.

THIS MEANS **WAR**

EW **VISITS THE SET OF AN EPIC BATTLE 10 YEARS IN THE MAKING, PITTING EARTH'S MIGHTIEST HEROES AGAINST THE INTERGALACTIC WARLORD THANOS IN *AVENGERS: INFINITY WAR*. NOT EVERYONE WILL MAKE IT OUT ALIVE.** *By Anthony Breznican*

With the Wakandan army at their backs, White Wolf (Sebastian Stan), Black Widow (Scarlett Johansson), Captain America (Chris Evans), the Hulk (Mark Ruffalo), Okoye (Danai Gurira) and Black Panther (Chadwick Boseman) lead the charge. War Machine (Don Cheadle) and Falcon (Anthony Mackie) fly support.

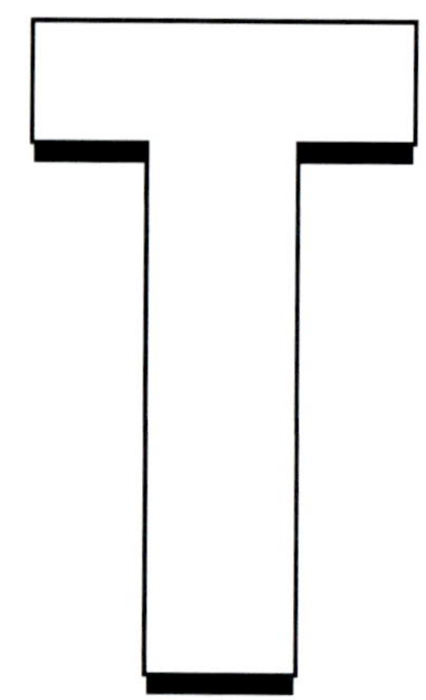

THE SKY IS A RAGING SEA OF GRAY STORM clouds, and a faraway rumble rolls across the countryside like something gigantic colliding with the other side of Earth.

Thor and Captain America are standing on an African savanna beside a sparkling river, back-to-back for the first time in ages, each reunited with his old friend while wielding new weapons. Cap's red-white-and-blue shield is gone, replaced by a pair of vibranium gauntlets (courtesy of Black Panther's genius little sister Shuri), while Thor swings a mystical ax known as Stormbreaker, a supersize upgrade from his demolished hammer Mjolnir.

The skyline of Wakanda's capital city stands in the distance, and Cap and Thor are among hundreds of tribal warriors from throughout the nation, gathered at the river's edge to join the heroes in facing down a horde of synthetic-alien demons known as the Outriders. This is the flash-point of an epic battle in *Avengers: Infinity War,* and it's not just about saving the world this time—Earth's mightiest heroes, and some from much farther away, are gathered together to try to save the entire universe from a genocidal tyrant who'd like to kill off half of it.

No pressure.

Right now the cast and crew of the biggest team-up in superhero-movie history have a real-world problem to confront. The river is fake, of course. It was dug out of this grassy horse field near Atlanta, and giant pumps at either end recirculate the water as needed. The savanna is a lot closer to Savannah than any plains of Africa. The fictional skyscrapers of Wakanda are represented for now by a green screen, and the Outrider attackers are actors in motion-capture suits.

But the approaching rainstorm happens to be real. Chris Hemsworth lowers his battle-ax and looks off into the distance. The God of Thunder is in a race against his own superpower.

If the production is close enough to see a flash, union rules stipulate that everyone has to take shelter for 30 minutes. They might not have that long before the downpour begins, so directors Anthony and Joe Russo are hurrying to get their shots while supervising multiple camera units on different scenes.

For instance, on the other side of the river, Sebastian Stan's Bucky Barnes, now known to his Wakandan friends as White Wolf, is laying waste to Outriders while Rocket (in the form of Sean Gunn as the physical stand-in for the CG space creature voiced by Bradley Cooper) distracts him with banter.

"How much for the gun?" the furry dealmaker asks, admiring the firepower clutched by Bucky's mechanical limb.

"It's not for sale."

"Okay, how much for the arm? The arm?" Rocket persists.

The strength of *Infinity War* is not just in assembling what appears to be the entire roster of Marvel's cinematic superheroes in common cause, it's in pairing the oddest of couples. Even Hemsworth and Chris Evans, on the other side of the water, are conspiring to make Thor and Cap's reunion just a little bit weirder.

▲
Doctor Strange (Benedict Cumberbatch), Tony Stark (Robert Downey Jr.), Bruce Banner (Mark Ruffalo) and Strange's associate Wong (Benedict Wong) stare up at the New York City skyline.

◀
Rocket Raccoon (Bradley Cooper) and Mantis (Pom Klementieff) treat Thor (Chris Hemsworth) aboard their spaceship.

But before they can complete their takes, lightning crackles nearby, followed by curtains of stinging rain that send the whole production stampeding for cover. *EW*'s day one on the set comes to an abrupt and muddy end.

THIS MOVIE IS A CULMINATION, A PUNCtuation mark on 10 years of superhero storytelling that changed the way movies are made. Kevin Feige, the president of Marvel Studios and the mastermind behind its interlocked universe of films (now nearing 20), says he wanted *Infinity War* and next year's still-untitled follow-up, which was shot at the same time, to also be pioneering.

"The notion of an ending, the notion of a finale, became very intriguing to us, in large part because you don't see it that often in this particular genre," he says. That doesn't mean there won't be any more movies. Disney has announced at least 10 more films set in the Marvel Cinematic Universe.

But Feige is aware that the only thing that could kill the franchise is complacency, if they don't keep evolving and engaging moviegoers. The danger is lack of surprise.

Some heroes are just getting started: Chadwick Boseman's Black Panther, Benedict Cumberbatch's Doctor Strange and Tom Holland's Spider-Man. Other heroes have had multifilm arcs, with actors who have hinted they're ready to move on, or at least step back. One of them is Robert Downey Jr., whose charisma in the first chapter, 2008's *Iron Man*, was a key building block in this expanding universe.

"Clearly Kevin is, in addition to everything else, an excellent, almost clairvoyant troubleshooter," Downey tells *EW*.

According to *Infinity War*'s screenwriters Christopher Markus and Stephen McFeely, who cowrote all three Captain America movies, some heroes may simply get to ride off into the sunset. Others may fall in battle.

Some things must end. And the idea of clearing away some to make way for others is the plan of the villain Thanos, a godlike galactic warlord played via motion capture by Josh Brolin. Ever since the first Avengers film featured his smirking purple face as a post-credit surprise, he has been built up as the ultimate tyrant.

"He's from a planet called Titan that's no longer inhabited because of things that he thought he could help prevent, and he was not allowed to do that," Feige says. "He vowed not to let that happen again."

Since Thanos is a glass-half-full guy, he sees his mission as saving half the universe. But to do that he wants to kill off the other half. "That's either genius or horrific, depending on your point of view, and most of our points of view say it's pretty horrific," Feige says.

Cosmic genocide is no easy task, so to accomplish his goal, Thanos needs his legion of genetically engineered Outriders to help him acquire the six Infinity Stones. When combined into a single mystical gauntlet, those gems will allow him to bend time, space, energy and the laws of physics and reality. Only one has yet to be revealed—the orange Soul Stone.

"He's on a hunt," Joe Russo says. "We're using a bit of a '90s-heist genre component. Thanos is on a smash-and-grab, and everybody's trying to catch up the whole movie."

Doctor Strange has the green Time Stone, Benicio Del Toro's the Collector has the red Reality Stone, and the intergalactic police force Nova Corps has the purple Power Stone, while Tom Hiddleston's Loki has snatched the blue Space Stone. The yellow Mind Stone is embedded in the forehead of Paul Bettany's

▲
T'Challa prepares for battle amid the warriors of Wakanda.

◀
Paralyzed no more, James Rhodes shares a moment with Steve Rogers and Natasha Romanoff.

Vision and was a key component to bring him to life. It's doubtful he can survive long without it.

THAT BRINGS US TO *EW'S* DAY TWO, THIS TIME in the woods on the same equestrian ranch, doubling as the Wakandan jungle. Cap, Black Panther, Scarlett Johansson's Black Widow and Mark Ruffalo's Hulk are protecting an ailing Vision, who collapses in agony as Thanos and his gauntlet of space gems draws near.

"Vision is a living MacGuffin," Anthony Russo says. "[H]is life is in conflict with Thanos's goals, so something's got to give."

Stalking the heroes through the overgrowth is Proxima Midnight, one of the warriors Thanos kidnapped when they were young to train as bloodthirsty lieutenants, just as he did with his estranged "children" Gamora (Zoe Saldana) and Nebula (Karen Gillan).

"Cap makes the decision to bring [Vision] here to Wakanda," Anthony Russo says. "Earth is making its last stand to keep the stone from Thanos. It's the best place to make your last stand."

An important part of the lore of Wakanda is that the fictional African nation is so powerful it has never been successfully invaded. That's no longer the case, but Black Panther and his people are doing their best to push Thanos's army back out again. "It's never been conquered, but that doesn't mean it hasn't been challenged," Boseman says.

This is all new for Okoye, Danai Gurira's head of the Dora Milaje, Wakanda's special forces. She just got used to foreigners; now she's fighting alongside talking raccoons and aliens. "Change is scary," the actress says. "But I think the learning curve is to become a citizen of the world versus a citizen of Wakanda."

Still, T'Challa and Okoye welcome Cap, Vision and the others as friends, as allies, to their homeland. As we saw at the end of *Black Panther,* the new king wants his country to stand up for more than itself.

"They trust each other," Boseman says of Panther and Cap. The actor points to his gift of Shuri's (Letitia Wright) claw shields, forged from Wakanda's sacred natural resource. "His shield was already made from vibranium anyway. So it's just an extension of what he already had. This time, actually giving it to him, as opposed to..." Boseman shrugs—the materials for the old shield were likely taken, not offered. "Me actually giving it to him is a testament to our relationship and trust."

BESIDE THE WOODLAND SET IS A LAKE, where a falcon can often be spotted pulling fish out of the mirrored water. That's Falcon with a capital F—Anthony Mackie's mechanical-winged hero.

During breaks between shots, he takes out a rod and reel and ventures down to the water's edge to catch dinner. Mackie says his character isn't comfortable in Wakanda. He actually doesn't trust a lot of the other heroes and has a grudge against Iron Man and Black Panther from the events of *Captain America: Civil War.*

Now, as he puts it, Marvel's heroes are trying to "get the band back together." As he talks, he gets a tug on his line and reels in a largemouth bass. But Mackie looks at the fish with concern. This fish has been caught before. There's another hook from a broken line embedded in its throat. Mackie tries to remove it but can't.

"Lucky I caught him. I should just keep him and cook him," the actor says. Instead he lowers the fish to the water and lets the creature swim free. "If it ain't killed him yet, it ain't gonna kill him," Mackie says.

For Marvel's superheroes, that's the best they can hope for too.

▲ The final third of *Infinity War* takes place in Wakanda. Here, Falcon sweeps in over the battle.

◀ The Sorcerer Supreme stands with his new allies as they confront the reality of Thanos's arrival.

Thanos prepares to unleash the powers of the Infinity Gauntlet on Earth.

BAD TO THE BONE

SPORTING A FEW HUNDRED POUNDS OF PURPLE CGI MUSCLE, JOSH BROLIN BREATHES LIFE INTO AN INTERSTELLAR WARLORD WITH A SERIOUS GRUDGE AGAINST HUMANITY. *By Anthony Breznican*

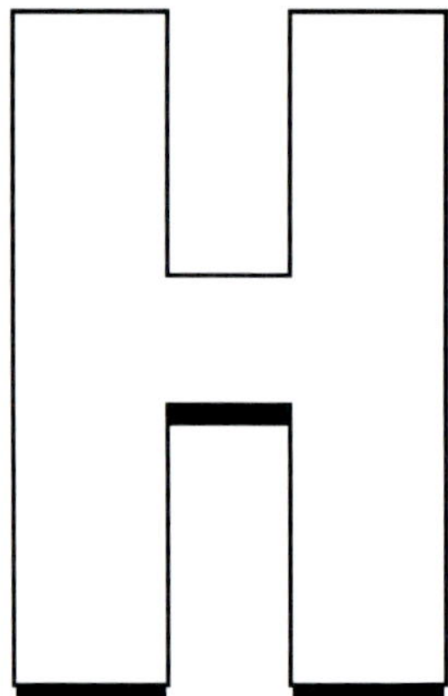

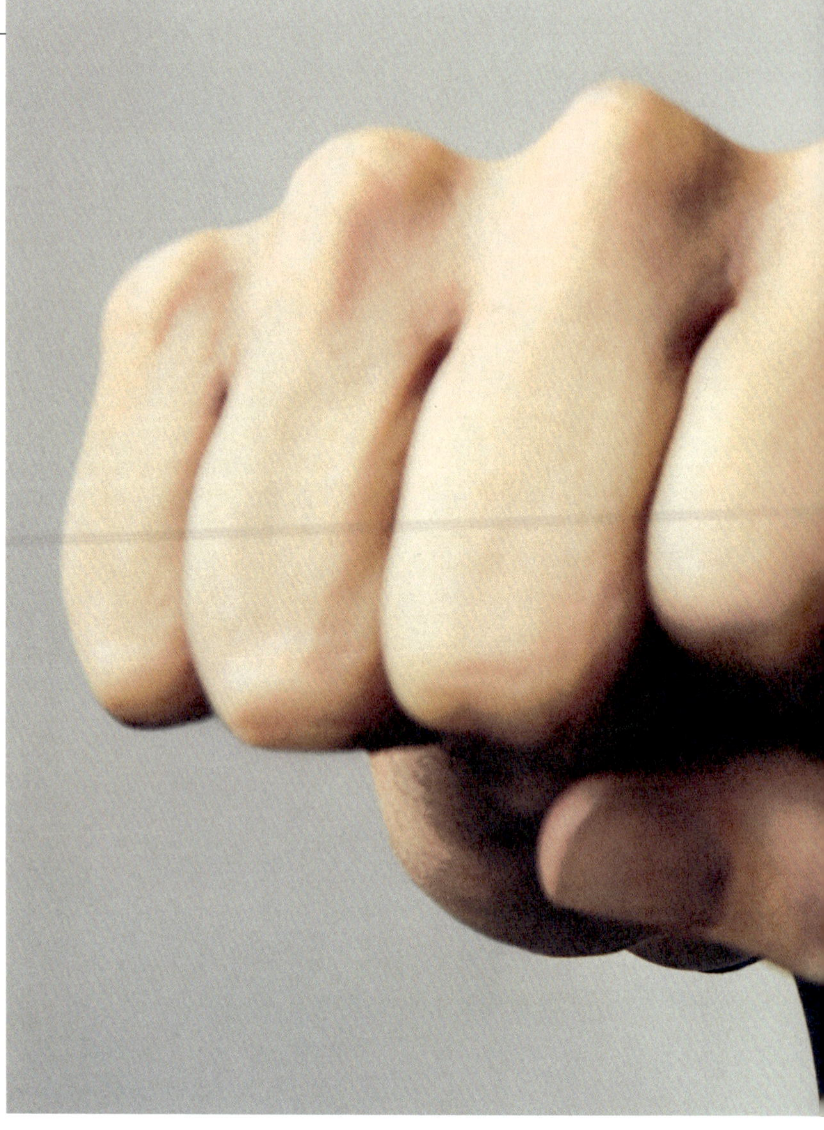

HE'S A POWERFUL BEING FROM AN EXTINCT alien world that ended up destroying itself. Venturing through deep space, he arrives wielding unfathomable cosmic powers on an idealistic quest to save the galaxy. In another story that might describe a beloved superhero. In the MCU he is one of the darkest villains imaginable—Thanos, the Mad Titan, who believes the only way to save half the universe is by exterminating the other half. We first glimpsed the violet-skinned monstrosity at the end of 2012's *The Avengers,* which set him up as the Final Boss of these interlocked movies.

In *Avengers: Infinity War,* Josh Brolin's character Thanos becomes the central focus, and we'll see his younger years on Titan, witnessing the forces that wiped out his homeland and sent him on a mission to "save" the universe through mass destruction. To do so, Thanos has been trying to acquire the Infinity Stones that, when added to his gauntlet, will allow him to bend time, space and reality to his will. *EW* spoke with Brolin about bringing to life Marvel's "biggest bad" yet and whether there is something human in someone so bent on destruction.

You're playing a towering space tyrant. Does Thanos have a correlation to a type of person who exists in the real world?

That's an interesting question because I'm the least-educated person you'll ever meet when it comes to this stuff. I knew nothing about Thanos. Nothing. And it was great. I got to start from scratch. I bring that up, because you go, "Who is he?" Kind of an amalgamation of people, to me. "And who specifically?" You want to really go out on a limb. Because it's not okay to actually parallel with people. But he doesn't divert from his intention at all. Who could be like that? [*Laughs*] But at the same time, you feel for him. You want to write him off as insane, and yet what he's doing makes sense, if you break it [down].

He's bringing order, right?

You think of overpopulation and killing half the universe in order to save the other half and all this kind of stuff. It actually makes scientific sense. You have this struggle watching him. It's this love-hate thing, you know? So I don't know.... Who in our society do we love and hate?

He looks like a thug. Like a Neanderthal. He has that swagger of someone who uses his strength to intimidate.

And that's great. And that's your perception of it. You see this lughead and this guy who you pigeonhole right from the first cosmetic reaction to him. And what I see is this in this guy's eyes. This super, super, super intelligence. There's this constant contrasting thing about this Neanderthalic lughead who's way more intelligent than anybody else in the movie, by far.

Is he also the abusive father? We know he kidnapped Gamora (Zoe Saldana) and Nebula (Karen Gillan) and trained them to be child soldiers.

They're tools to him.

Josh Brolin posed for *People* in July 2017 at Disney's D23 celebration in Anaheim, Calif.

Is he cold the whole way through, or does he feel any affection for them?
Yeah. I do think he does. You see the relationship with Gamora and you see that evolve.... When [directors Joe and Anthony Russo] came up to me after we had done maybe three quarters of the film, they said, "It wasn't necessarily intended that you feel for this guy as much as you do." Obviously he has a grand plan, like somebody who's pulling in kids for their own selfish bloodshed. But he has a capacity to love very much and very deeply.

You need that for a character like this. If he's just a cackling madman bent on destruction, it's less interesting.
It's like Dan White, man. [That's the true-life, mentally unbalanced politician turned killer Brolin played in 2008's biopic *Milk*.] If he just had somebody to listen to him or he just had [help].... You kind of get that with Thanos a little bit.

What is it that damaged Thanos? Where does all this pain and anger come from?
He's different from his family. They're all Titans, and they all look similar, but he was born deformed. You see how he grew up. You see he was like the Quasimodo of this time, or if you've ever read *Perfume* [Patrick Süskind's 1985 novel about a serial killer who craves beautiful scents but is disgusted by the smell of humanity], it's a great parallel to Thanos. He stuck out. He was an anomaly. He was a freak. And that lent to this apparent insanity. And yet [his actions] start to make sense.

GLOVE STORY

Eagle-eyed viewers got their first look at the Infinity Gauntlet in 2011's *Thor*, where it made a blink-and-you'll-miss-it appearance as a trophy in Odin's weapons vault. (It turned out to be a fake, as revealed in 2017's *Thor: Ragnarok*.) The six Infinity Stones that give the Gauntlet its vast power have been popping up for years, with Thanos determined to possess them all. Here's what we know thus far about each one. **BY GLENN GREENBERG**

• THE ORB, THE POWER STONE
First Appearance *Guardians of the Galaxy* (2014)
Function Grants its user life-destroying power on a cosmic scale.
Last Seen In the custody of the intergalactic peacekeeping force Nova Corps, on the planet Xandar.

• THE MIND STONE
First Appearance *The Avengers,* as part of Loki's scepter (2012)
Function Grants its user the ability to control minds.
Last Seen Used in the creation of the Vision (Paul Bettany) in 2015's *Avengers: Age of Ultron*. The stone still resides in his forehead as of 2016's *Captain America: Civil War.*

• THE TESSERACT, THE SPACE STONE
First Appearance *Thor* (2011)
Function Grants its user the power over space, enabling Loki (Tom Hiddleston) to lead an alien invasion force to Earth through a portal in 2012's *The Avengers*.
Last Seen Glimpsed by Loki during the destruction of Asgard in *Thor: Ragnarok*.

• THE AETHER, THE REALITY STONE
First Appearance *Thor: The Dark World* (2013)
Function Can reshape reality—Malekith, Lord of the Dark Elves (Christopher Eccleston), tried to use it to plunge the universe into total darkness.
Last Seen Given to the Collector (Benicio Del Toro) for safekeeping.

• THE EYE OF AGAMOTTO, THE TIME STONE
First Appearance *Doctor Strange* (2016)
Function Grants its user the power to manipulate the flow of time.
Last Seen In the custody of the Masters of the Mystic Arts.

• THE SOUL STONE
First Appearance Yet to appear
Function If it's anything like its comic-book counterpart, it may have the ability to collect and control people's souls and trap them inside itself.

PHOTOGRAPH BY JUSTIN FANTL

TO *INFINITY* AND **BEYOND**

CODIRECTING BROTHERS JOE AND ANTHONY RUSSO FIRST MARSHALED MARVEL'S SUPERTROOPS IN 2014'S ELECTRIFYING *CAPTAIN AMERICA: THE WINTER SOLDIER*. BUT THE EXPONENTIALLY MASSIVE *AVENGERS: INFINITY WAR* REQUIRED AN EVEN MORE ELABORATE BATTLE PLAN. *By Gina McIntyre*

Director Joe Russo (left background, with his brother Anthony) talks to actors Sebastian Stan (left foreground) and Chris Evans on the set of *Captain America: Civil War.*

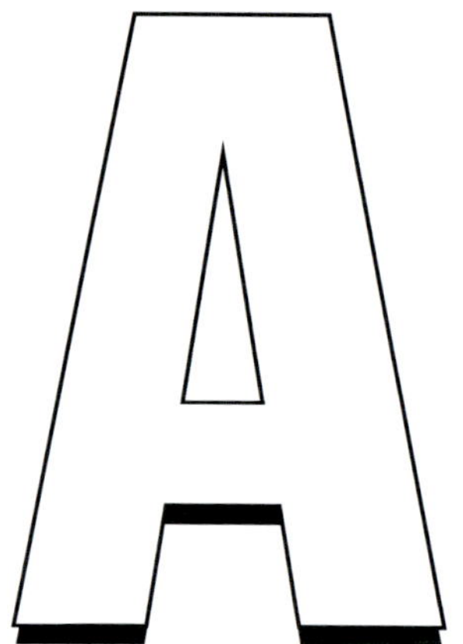

Joe Russo (left) and Anthony with Frank Grillo (who played the villain Crossbones) on the *Captain America: Civil War* set.

ANTHONY RUSSO WAS MIDWAY THROUGH A sentence when an ear-piercing sound brought him up short. Joe Russo heard it too. But the other party on the line? Nothing. "It had to be Thanos, because I've never heard a sound like that," Joe Russo said, referring to the cosmic villain bedeviling the universe in their new film *Avengers: Infinity War*. "Or," offered his brother, "after shooting for a year straight, we're collectively insane now."

To be fair, the monumental undertaking that is directing the Biggest Avengers Movie Ever would be enough to maybe make anyone hear things that weren't there. But if any two people would be prepared to helm the massive superhero adventure, it's the Russos. After cutting their teeth in television on such critically acclaimed series as *Arrested Development* and *Community* and the 2002 indie movie *Welcome to Collinwood*, the fraternal directing partners graduated to blockbusters with 2014's *Captain America: The Winter Soldier*. And they've remained in the Marvel universe ever since.

Paying homage to classics such as *The French Connection*, the Russos dropped Chris Evans's upstanding hero into the morass of modern politics with a smart thriller that pushed the MCU in a clever new direction. On the heels of that success, they made what was then the biggest movie for the blockbuster factory—*Captain America: Civil War*, which pitted about 74 beloved heroes (Okay, more like 12, but who's counting?) against one another for the battle of the century. But even that roster pales in comparison to *Infinity War*, which features virtually ever major star in the galaxy and scales up the action further than ever before.

We caught up with the directors as they were putting the finishing touches on the new Biggest Avengers Movie Ever (which was shot back-to-back with next year's follow-up) to find out how it feels to assemble all those superheroes, how they balanced building a compelling adventure with crafting important character moments and how they're liking Chris Evans's newly bearded Captain America.

This is the culmination of a decade of some of the most successful blockbuster moviemaking in history. How much pressure did you feel?

JOE RUSSO You have to expel all pressure from your life. You can't make decisions based on what you think people want to see...because it clouds your judgment. You can't please all the fans. You go online, you go on Twitter—everybody wants something different from these movies. What we do on each film, we try to appease ourselves. We're comic-book fans. I still have my comic-book collection that I've had for 30 years in my closet. We grew up emotionally attached to this material. We love these characters. We try to make films that appeal to us, and we hope that everyone else loves it as much as we do.

How difficult is it to service so many characters and at the same time tell a clear, concise story?

ANTHONY RUSSO It's a real challenge, but Joe and I have always thrived on creative challenges. Joe and I have always been drawn to ensemble storytelling. Part of the reason we like ensembles is we love density of storytelling, the ability to approach a narrative or a movie from various points of view....We had more characters than we ever had to deal with before in a movie like this, but one of the great things we had to work with is that most of these characters have been alive in the MCU. There have been stories told about them. Audiences have invested in them emotionally. We can build upon all that capital....We don't have to do a lot of work building up who these people are to the audience.

JR A movie like this couldn't exist outside of the Marvel universe because if you had to tell all the backstories and all the character history of each person in this movie

STORIES THAT YOU DISCOVER AS A CHILD, YOU HAVE AN INCREDIBLE EMOTIONAL ATTACHMENT TO"

—JOE RUSSO

it would be a 14-hour film. That's why the film is creatively unique. There's not a lot of movies that have been able to do that, to build upon a larger mosaic.

The tone of, say, *Guardians of the Galaxy* is very different from the *Captain America* movies. How did you reconcile those differences to find the tone for this film?

JR Again, that is part of what's exciting about it for us. We feel like mad scientists in a laboratory experimenting, pouring different beakers into one another and hoping things don't explode. You pull everybody closer to one another in a way. You pull the Guardians closer to the *Avengers'* tone. You pull the Avengers closer to the *Guardians'* tone.... It's a different interpretation of the Guardians than you've seen. It's a different interpretation of the Avengers than you've seen. Our motto as we have proceeded on these movies is keeping it fresh and surprising for the audience. I don't want to go in knowing exactly what I'm going to get.

How did you set up Thanos to believably make him the greatest threat that the universe has ever seen?

JR Josh Brolin brings a gravitas and an intensity and a confidence and—this will be tricky for people to understand until they see the movie—a vulnerability and a warmth. This movie is told from the point of Thanos. It's a unique film in that way. Working in a narrative mosaic as complex as the Marvel universe, you can actually take a film and ascribe it to a villain. I hope this goes a long way toward any villain issues people have with the Marvel films. He doesn't pull any punches, and the stakes are life and death for him. His goal is a lifelong goal, and it's in direct conflict to what the Avengers and the Guardians want. He's willing to fight to the death for it, Thanos.

You shot the film exclusively with IMAX cameras. Why?

JR We felt like we wanted the biggest canvas possible to tell [this] story. IMAX is unique to modern cinema, and we felt it was an incredible opportunity to really exploit the scale of that format. Frankly, some of the alien characters, including Thanos, are very large and the top to bottom that IMAX brings complements the size of the characters in the frame.

You've staged two of Marvel's greatest action sequences—the *Winter Soldier* car chase and the airport battle scene in *Civil War*. How do you top those?

AR We approach action the same way we approach storytelling. You can't really just go, "We're going to do the greatest action sequence ever!" You have to find it within the movie, within the storytelling. In the same way we want to challenge a character on an emotional level, on a dramatic level, we want to challenge them on an action level. The whole airport sequence in *Civil War* was all built around character.

JR These [*Avengers*] movies in particular are heading toward the greatest battles of all time in the Marvel universe because of the amount of heroes involved and because of the formidableness of the villain. Hopefully people [will] find it as thrilling as the car chase or the airport sequence.

They can marvel at Cap's new facial hair.

AR We do love the beard.

5

A FRIEND FROM WORK!

Thor: Ragnarok, 2017

The first Marvel limited comic-book series, Contest of Champions, introduced the idea of heroes battling in the arena of the Grandmaster (played onscreen by Jeff Goldblum). *Ragnarok* brought that idea to the screen a quarter-century later on the planet Sakaar. When Thor (Chris Hemsworth) saunters into the arena and encounters the Hulk (Mark Ruffalo), he's much relieved—but not for long. Hulk isn't big on workplace camaraderie. For Loki (Tom Hiddleston), who had suffered the green giant's wrath before, it's a moment to treasure.

THE **BEST** OF THE **BEST**

FROM INTERSTELLAR DANCE-OFFS TO SHAWARMA SMORGASBORDS, HERE ARE THE FUNNIEST, COOLEST, MOST BADASS MOMENTS SINCE EARTH'S MIGHTIEST HEROES BEGAN TO ASSEMBLE. *By John Jackson Miller*

1
"I AM IRON MAN"
Iron Man, 2008

Secret identity? Save it for Bruce Wayne. Tony Stark (Robert Downey Jr.) wants the world to know he's added action hero to his billionaire/genius/playboy calling card. In the film's finale he proudly proclaims he's the guy inside the tin suit—at a press conference, no less—as gal Friday Pepper Potts (Gwyneth Paltrow) stands by.

2
LOOK OUT! HERE COMES THE SPIDER-MAN
Captain America: Civil War, 2016

Spidey (Tom Holland) swings into the MCU just as the Marvel heroes are squaring off for a superhero showdown. The amazing arachnid's arrival at the German airport makes for six heroes on each side—and a debut that impresses even Captain America (Chris Evans). But it's an insect, not an arachnid, that changes the odds, when Ant-Man (Paul Rudd) expands into his colossal Giant-Man incarnation!

3
ANOTHER WAY TO SETTLE THINGS
Guardians of the Galaxy, 2014

Everybody knows a superhero movie culminates in a climactic battle of good against evil. Everybody, that is, except Chris Pratt's goofy Star-Lord, who challenges his nemesis Ronan (Lee Pace) to a dance-off rather than the traditional amped-up fisticuffs. As Drax the Destroyer (Dave Bautista) says, "There are two types of beings in the universe: those who dance and those who do not." Wise words.

4
INTERROGATION, INTERRUPTED
The Avengers, 2012

Taking a call from the boss isn't always comfortable—even less so when you're being held prisoner. But Black Widow (Scarlett Johansson) demonstrates that it's a minor inconvenience—and that she's a force to be reckoned with—by wrecking her captors while S.H.I.E.L.D.'s Agent Coulson (Clark Gregg) is on hold.

Blauflug

4

RIDE OF THE VALKYRIE

Thor: Ragnarok, 2017

After the Valkyries of Asgard were defeated by Hela (Cate Blanchett), sole survivor Brunnhilde fled to Sakaar to drink and forget her pain. But "Scrapper 142" (Tessa Thompson) couldn't keep away from the fight for long. Thor wisely seeks her aid to reclaim their homeland from the goddess of death—and the Valkyrie eventually jumps at the chance to get a bit of revenge for the deaths of her comrades.

WAKANDA JOINS THE WORLD

Black Panther, 2018

In the mid-credits scene inspired by the "I Am Iron Man" moment, T'Challa (Chadwick Boseman) addresses the United Nations—and prepares to spring a surprise on the whole planet, revealing his nation's technological advancement. Long live the king.

OPENING BOAT RAID

Captain America: The Winter Soldier, 2014

Batroc the Leaper might be one of the sillier villains in Marvel's Silver Age stable—as the name suggests, in the comics he just leaps around, taunting Captain America with epithets spoken in French. But his hijacking of a S.H.I.E.L.D. satellite-launch ship gave Cap and Black Widow the chance to start *The Winter Soldier* in full caper mode—and trade a few quips along the way.

PUNY GOD!

The Avengers, 2012

Tom Hiddleston's Loki is a man of many words. Hulk, not so much. "I am a god, you dull creature, and I will not be bullied by..." Thor's power-mad little brother doesn't get to complete his thought once the mean, green alter ego of Dr. Bruce Banner (Mark Ruffalo) begins to swing him around like a rag doll. To finish the beatdown, Hulk offers a derisive aside about the Asgardian. Though, in fairness, most folks are pretty puny compared to a Hulk.

A BITE AFTER WORK

The Avengers, 2012

The gang's gotta eat, and there's nothing like saving the planet from hordes of Chitauri invaders to help work up an appetite. After Tony offhandedly mentions trying the Middle Eastern dish shawarma to his pals during the fight, the Avengers are seen sharing a meal at a local diner in the final post-credits scene. Fortunately there was a place still open after the destruction. No word on whether Tony picked up the tab or where they stashed Loki during their chow-down.

6

7

8

9

MIGH

TIEST HEROES

IRON GIANT

TONY STARK HIMSELF—ACTOR ROBERT DOWNEY JR.—OPENS UP ON A DECADE OF IRON MAN, SCIENCE BROS AND WHAT LIES AHEAD. *By Anthony Breznican*

Tony Stark suits up in the Bleeding Edge Iron Man armor, complete with rocket thrusters that jut out from his arms and back.

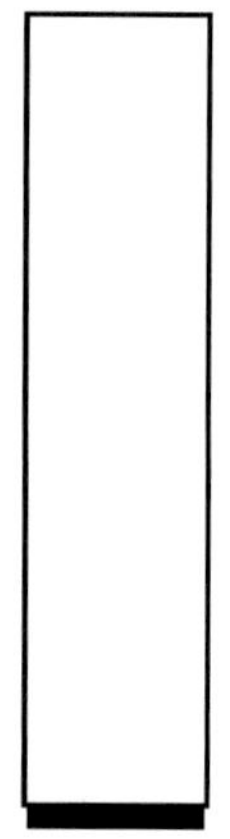

***IRON MAN* WAS THE BIG BANG THAT GAVE** birth to the entire Marvel Cinematic Universe back in 2008, and Robert Downey Jr. was the spark that ignited it. Back then, Tony Stark was considered a B-list superhero, and Downey was reaching for a comeback after recovering from addiction, which threatened not only his career but his life. Both proved to be stratospheric stories of success and redemption. Over the past decade, Downey has taken the billionaire playboy philanthropist from selfish to selfless, from rule breaker to rule enforcer. With *Avengers: Infinity War,* the character is still seeking a home in the world he keeps saving from oblivion. In conversation Downey is as freewheeling as a man in an iron suit, swept by currents as he glides from one point in the sky to the next. Here's an edited version of where he took us.

In the last few movies, Tony has been trying to find a way out of the hero game. Is that still where he is?

Well, let's compare him to me. If I was going to not be playing Tony for the next 10 years, I wouldn't be doing it with no plan of what I would do instead. I don't think Tony is idle; I think he is wondering.... Look, when he tried to make a suit of armor around the world [in *Avengers: Age of Ultron*], that didn't pan out so well.

If the suits do the heavy lifting without him, what's Tony's role?

I always feel bad for guys who still haven't gotten their relationship together or procreated, and they're looking at the back nine. Because you kind of go, like, "Are you going to be that dad who people are wondering if the kid's grandpa came to the soccer game?" So I think there's probably some of that going on.

Stark's personal life was put aside in recent movies.

It was hard to thread Pepper [Potts, Stark's longtime Stark Industries colleague and girlfriend played by Gwyneth Paltrow] through every story that Tony was in, so we took opportunities to say, "We're taking a break, and it's my fault." [*Laughs*] Now he and Pepper have kind of locked it up. We were talking about them living in some eco-lodge together, but then we thought, "Eh, anytime they move somewhere [villains] just blow it up, so no one's gonna believe that it'll stay long."

With so many characters in *Infinity War*, I wasn't sure how personal their stories could be here.

Pepper remains the heart of the story. I think we wanted to get back to that reality. Not just for them, but let's really see how that can add to the stakes and the something-worth-fighting-for of it all.

Your team is Iron Man, Doctor Strange and warrior-librarian Wong. Then Bruce Banner crashes to Earth.

I love how [Benedict] Cumberbatch just comes in and kind of draws flaming circles anywhere and can basically step into your movie. That's fun. And we wanted to keep a little bit of the science-bros thing alive even though [Mark] Ruffalo has been on such an amazing Banner/Hulk journey himself. I really enjoyed getting to know and work with and play around with Benedict as Strange. Benedict Wong also, by the way, is fantastic.

Spider-Man, Tom Holland's Peter Parker, also lends a hand.

I think [Marvel] is smart: "Oh yeah, we like the Parker/Stark thing. So let's keep them at close quarters as long as we can." Someone under your tutelage is now firing on all cylinders, but you're responsible for bringing them into deeper water.

What do we need to know about the threat they're facing?

Believe me, I'm tired of every movie, you know, "It's the end! It's Armageddon! It's the be-all, end-all, forever!" And then it's...not. This one actually is. [*Laughs*] They're not kidding. This is a heads-will-roll scenario.

The Iron Man of the comics had a different personality from the way you played him. How much of yourself did you put into him?

I wonder. [*Pause*] I ain't him, I'll tell you that flat out. There's always a bit of a burn-off period when they run out of call sheets for me. I'm just a f---ing actor. I'm just a guy who does have a very interesting past, who does not regret it, who wished to shut the door on it. I think that that translates.

I think it does.

If you're going to do that, then why don't you infuse it with as much of your own soul? It's funny because in some ways Chris Evans is the least like the character he's portrayed, but he does it so convincingly. When I'm shooting scenes with him as Cap, I don't even see Chris anymore. It's gotten that nutty. So I feel like I'm friends with Chris Evans, but I work with Captain America.

Is it important to you as a storyteller for Tony's arc to reach a conclusion?

I think the trouble is the endlessness. We're going to pull out the stops and look to do stuff that we go, "Oh, but if we do that, that's very, very definitive." Well, great. Let's get definitive for a change. The audience can feel what we're feeling, because we're like a family now. Ten years later we're, like, hanging out and having lunch and kind of wondering when the draft is going to come in, which one of us bites it and when.

That's the cost of going to war.

We're going somewhere. Far, far away. And

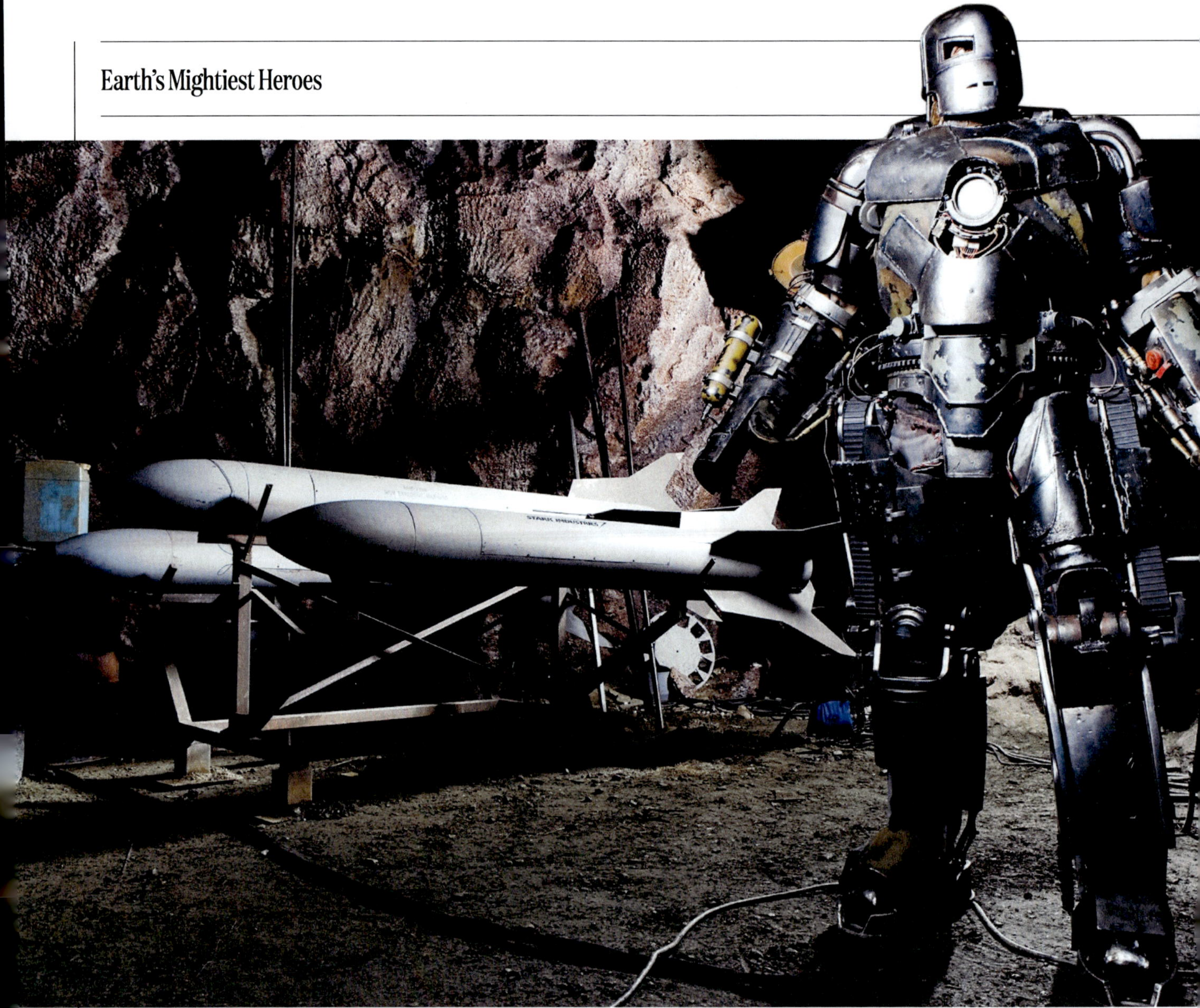

the idea, too, this time is rather than how do we set our battlements and what's our plan, we just have to bring the fight to wherever the fight is going to be. There's a lot more individuation. It's like a relationship. At this point, for the most part, the Avengers can think through what they do and don't have to...waste time by double-checking with everybody.

***Black Panther* struck quite a nerve. What do you suppose Tony will make of that whole world?**

Well, a technologically advanced country is probably something that he wishes in a way would benefit humanity without creating more infighting. I think that's what he would hope for America. That's what he would hope for the world. I think to him, he would view it as a potentially utopian model.

Is this the kind of thing you'd like to have be a part of your life and career for the next 20 to 30 years? Or are you feeling like it's good to maybe have this be a chapter of your life and move on?

I'm definitely a hang-up-your-jersey-before-they-boo-you-off-the-court-type guy, just because I still have an appropriate fear of embarrassment.... Who knows, man? This whole thing, it's like being in a rock band. You go, like, "Wait a minute, I was on my mother's couch, and now we're selling out stadiums." There's no way I could have said I planned this. In fact, you just literally suited up, you showed up, you did the next right thing, and some really cool stuff happened. Again you can't predict this stuff. It just means that you show up for what's put in front of you, and again if it's not my idea, it might actually lead to something pretty promising.

And what's next? You and your wife [producer Susan Downey] have the Team Downey production company. You're shooting 2019's *The Voyage of Doctor Dolittle.*

First of all, the missus is front and center with Joe Roth producing *Dolittle.* I still want to do *Pinocchio.* I have a million ideas, but I can tell you the God's honest truth. Having done *Avengers* 3 and 4 back-to-back, and now doing [*Dolittle,* in which Downey stars] . . . when I'm done with this, if you hear I'm not taking a break, call me and tell me I'm crazy.

▲
Left: Stark's Iron Man Mark I armor, used in 2008's *Iron Man* to escape imprisonment by the terrorist group the Ten Rings. Right: Tony teams up with James Rhodes (Don Cheadle), later War Machine in *Iron Man 2*.

◀
A battle-worn Stark in *Iron Man 3*, suffering from post-traumatic stress disorder, destroys all of his armor suits.

SUITING UP

From the somewhat modest Mark 1 to the intimidating Hulkbuster armor, Tony Stark has never stopped improving on his magnificent Iron Man machines. BY GLENN GREENBERG

Talk about humble beginnings. For Iron Man, it all started with the Mark 1, a crude, clunky, makeshift armor/life-support system cobbled together in a cave by an injured Tony Stark while he was being held captive by terrorists in Afghanistan. Since then, the brilliant inventor played by Robert Downey Jr. has built himself an assortment of suits that would seem to rival Imelda Marcos's infamous shoe collection—as of 2017's *Spider-Man: Homecoming,* he was up to the Mark 47, and there are more to come.

While all of the armors are based on Stark's patented Arc Reactor Technology, the billionaire superhero has constantly rethought and refined their capabilities and their looks—though he generally reverts to the traditional red-and-gold color scheme.

"The new suits are much more sophisticated [than the ones in the earlier movies]," says *Infinity War* costume designer Judianna Makovsky, who outfitted the armored Avenger in 2016's *Captain America: Civil War.* "They're more streamlined, and they have more functions."

Those functions are strictly story-driven, according to *Infinity War* visual-effects supervisor Dan DeLeeuw, a veteran of *Civil War* and 2013's *Iron Man 3.* "Each suit is tailored for what Tony needs it to do," he says.

Hence the Mark 44, more commonly known as the Hulkbuster armor, first revealed in 2015's *Avengers: Age of Ultron* and designed to take on you-know-who. An upgraded version of the Hulkbuster suit appears in *Infinity War* (right), and it's not the only new armor seen in the film. "We're pushing toward the next-generation armor in the comics, which can do some spectacular things," DeLeeuw says.

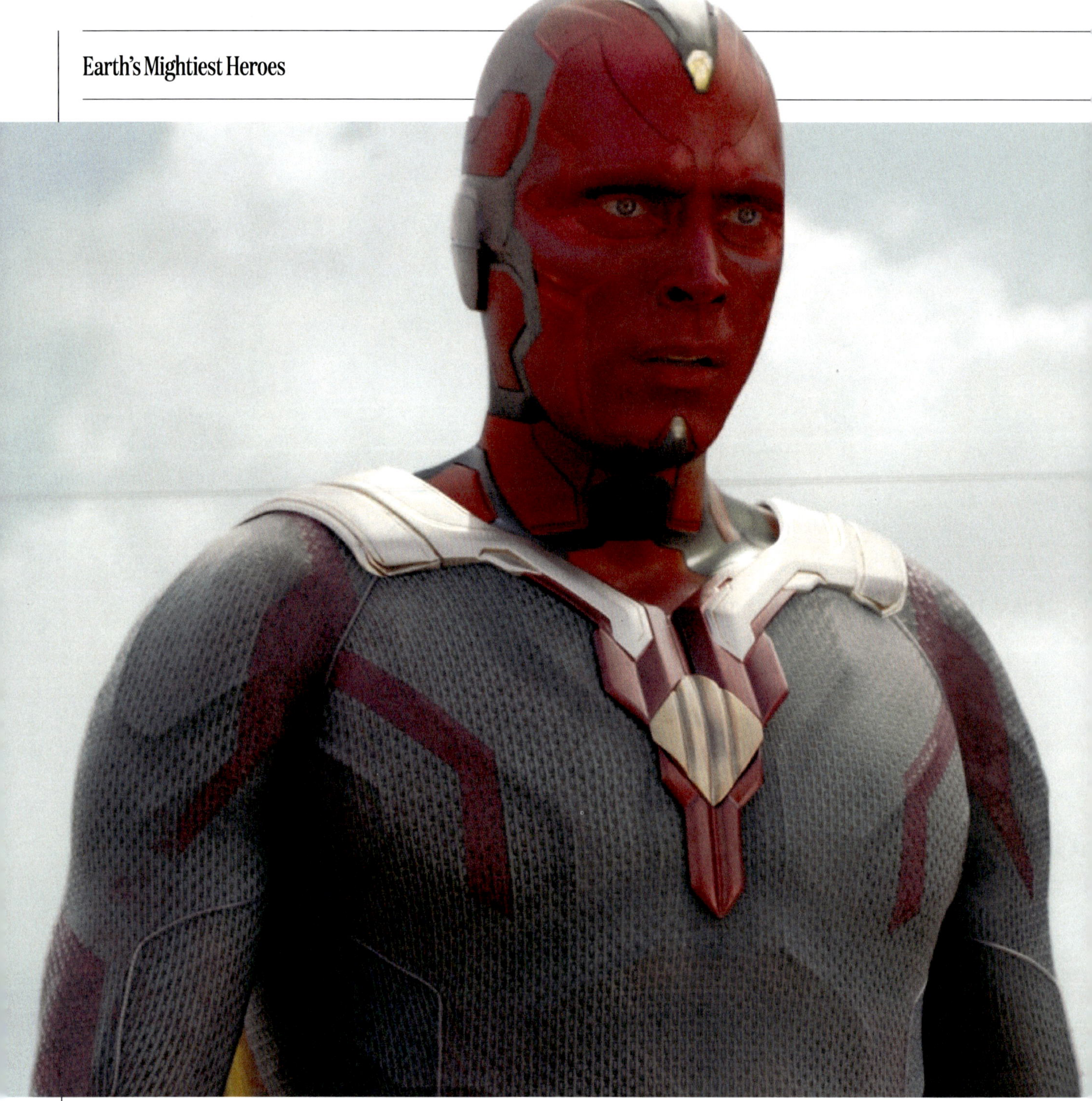

VISION *Paul Bettany*

HE WAS BORN FROM GOOD AND EVIL, AND HIS existence is guided by the Mind Stone housed in the center of his forehead. Which could spell trouble for Vision (Paul Bettany) given Thanos's plan to collect all of the infinity gems. "The stone's a real f---ing problem, yeah," Bettany says.

Vision began life as the disembodied intelligence J.A.R.V.I.S (named for the childhood butler who helped raise a young Tony Stark). In *Avengers: Age of Ultron,* he achieved corporeal form when a vibranium body designed to house Ultron's consciousness was stolen by science bros Stark (Robert Downey Jr.) and Bruce Banner (Mark Ruffalo). They uploaded J.A.R.V.I.S. and voilà: instant android superhero!

Driven by a mission to protect humankind, Vision then helped to defeat Ultron. Twice he has battled Scarlet Witch (Elizabeth Olsen) because of her alliances—first with Ultron and then Captain America. Despite it all, they fell in love. "I think there's a future for them, which is kind of beautiful," Bettany told *EW* last year.

That's assuming Vision survives the coming war. But according to Bettany, the the character has no problem sacrificing himself, should it come to that. "One man's life is not as important as the greater good," the actor says. Spoken like a true android hero. —***Sean Smith*** *(**additional reporting by Anthony Breznican**)*

HAWKEYE

Jeremy Renner

UNLIKE HIS FELLOW AVENGERS, STRAIGHT arrow Clint Barton (Jeremy Renner) must balance the demands of a normal life with his wife and children with the burden of defending the planet from evil forces. A devoted friend to Black Widow (Scarlett Johansson), whom he chose to recruit to S.H.I.E.L.D. rather than assassinate, the epic archer has been mind-controlled by Loki (Tom Hiddleston) and blasted by a HYDRA cannon. But the guy really knows how to rally and joined Captain America in the Civil War battle. Incarcerated at the underwater prison the Raft after that fight, he is freed by Cap (Chris Evans) and insists that he is retiring for good. But is he? Not every Marvel hero in the epic battle with Thanos will make it out alive, and Barton has had increasingly close calls before. If this does prove to be Hawkeye's last fight, there's little doubt that his final arrow will strike true. —*S.S.*

WAR MACHINE

Don Cheadle

***CIVIL WAR* ALMOST KILLED HIM. COLONEL JAMES RHODES (DON** Cheadle) has been a devoted friend of Tony Stark's since their youth. The liaison between Stark Industries and the military, Rhodes is in a constant battle to keep his billionaire friend on the straight and narrow. After battling Stark in an Iron Man prototype armor in *Iron Man 2*, Rhodes turned the suit over to the military, where it was modified into War Machine.

In *Civil War*, War Machine's loyalty to Tony nearly cost him his life. Hit by friendly fire from Vision during the battle, Rhodes plummeted to Earth and was left paralyzed. But it would be out of character for him to stay on the sidelines. "When you have somebody like Tony who is a master of tech...then you can walk again," Cheadle told *Good Morning America* last summer. When his friend needs him, War Machine never fails to step up. —*S.S.*

Tom Holland suits up as the Iron Spider in *Avengers: Infinity War.*

ALONG CAME A SPIDER

AFTER A SCENE-STEALING TURN IN *CAPTAIN AMERICA: CIVIL WAR,* TOM HOLLAND'S SPIDER-MAN IS BACK IN ACTION WITH THE AVENGERS AS THEY FACE A DEADLY COSMIC FOE IN HOPES OF—WHAT ELSE?—SAVING THE WORLD

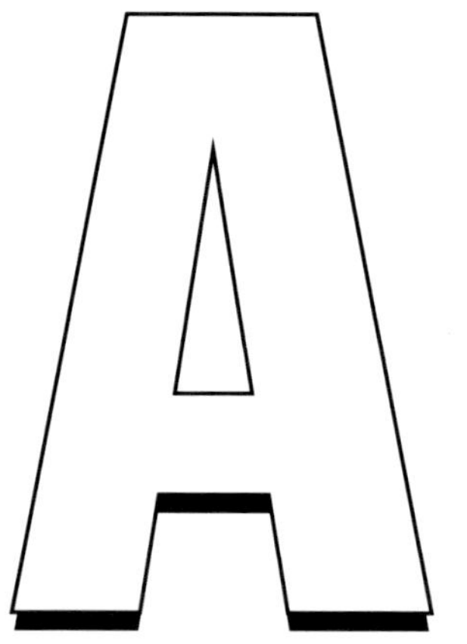

AT THE END OF *SPIDER-MAN: HOMECOMING,* last year's super-charming solo adventure featuring Brit Tom Holland as the teenage hero from Queens, Peter Parker is on top of the world. He's got a solid grasp of this good-guy racket after bringing Michael Keaton's villain to justice, and everything seems to be exactly as it should be. "He feels a massive sense of achievement," Holland says. "He's been offered the spot as an Avenger but turned it down." The teenage superhero had to learn quickly, and what he learned from his tussle with Vulture is that he wasn't quite ready for the big leagues. "He's just been living his best life, just a friendly neighborhood Spider-Man, looking out for the little guy, making sure everyone in his neighborhood is safe." Leave it to Thanos (Josh Brolin) to change all that. In *Avengers: Infinity War,* Peter finds himself drawn into a fight more epic than the young science whiz ever could have imagined—it's unquestionably the biggest test the wall-crawling webslinger has had to face. As his hero swings into the fray, Holland spoke to *EW*'s Anthony Breznican about the future.

How does Peter Parker enter this story?
So Peter Parker on that school bus is on his way to a school trip with his friends. He's just having a regular day in New York, and then suddenly his life is flipped upside down yet again. When this massive catastrophe happens in New York, his responsibility as a superhero for the people comes to light, and he has to join the Avengers that way.

He's pulled in whether he wants to be or not.
Yeah. It's his responsibility—with great power comes great responsibility—and he feels like he can't sit this one out. He feels compelled to join in and help save New York.

Will we see him outside of his neighborhood environment?
You'll definitely see him outside of his comfort zone. You'll be introduced to some new characters, and he'll have a lot of fun along the way. One thing that I was adamant about...with this film it's entertaining—his innocence, his lovable personality. So while some of the Avengers are maybe scared and a bit leery of the situation, he's wide-eyed and, if anything, enjoying the life of an Avenger for the first part. And then, as it's a bit more serious, he realizes the danger that he's in and maybe steps up again. But yeah, it's definitely an interesting arc for Peter Parker in this one.

It's not all fun and games, though. Thanos grabs Spidey by the neck and slams him down to the ground.
Not a fun scene to shoot. Not a fun scene to shoot.

Did you shoot that? Because I wondered how much of that was constructed by visual artists.
Josh wasn't there at that point. That was just me flopping on my back, pretending to be choked by an invisible Thanos. But yeah, it's fun; it's an interesting thing to play this character. Because on-set you're fighting someone, and you ask, "Who is it?" And they go, "We don't really want to tell you, because it's a secret." So this was fighting a tennis ball, having no idea what he would actually look like.

You were introduced to this universe as part of the team effort of *Captain America: Civil War.* Then you did your own Spider-Man movie. Is there a character arc for him in this story?
Actually, you know what? It is a deep arc. The nice thing...is that our characters are not the same as they were after we finished our first ones. So when I do *Spider-Man 2,* Peter Parker will have developed a little bit going into the second movie. So I don't have to pick it up right where I left off with the first one. It just allows us a bit more room to play, and also it makes them more interesting—the characters have changed just a little bit. And I like that. It gives me room to play and to find new things. In a film like this, where you're not a leading character, you can almost test the little light things you have, to see if it would work in a stand-alone. I know in *Civil War,* for me, that was like a big audition to the world. The world was really pleased with what I was doing. I just sort of did that again in *Spider-Man: Homecoming.*

I wonder if he begins to realize he can make a difference on a grand scheme, not just on a local level.
Whether he's able to deal with that level of pressure is something you'll have to wait and see. It definitely helps me find a new side for the character.

He's wearing the Iron Spider suit that we saw at the end of *Homecoming.* What new abilities does this suit offer him?
It does loads of new stuff, it's really cool, it's super-high-tech. Definitely an upgrade.

A lot of people want Shuri, Letitia Wright's character from *Black Panther,* and Peter Parker to meet. How do you feel Peter would respond to Wakanda?
I think Peter would love it. There are some great moments in the comics where Peter ends up there. And Letitia and I have become good friends. It's a nice thing about our little family we have with Marvel. Everyone gets along really well. I feel sorry for the Russo brothers when we're all on-set, because it's like trying to control a class of 12-year-olds. We're all just having so much fun.

Chris Evans and Scarlett Johansson costar in *Captain America: The Winter Soldier.*

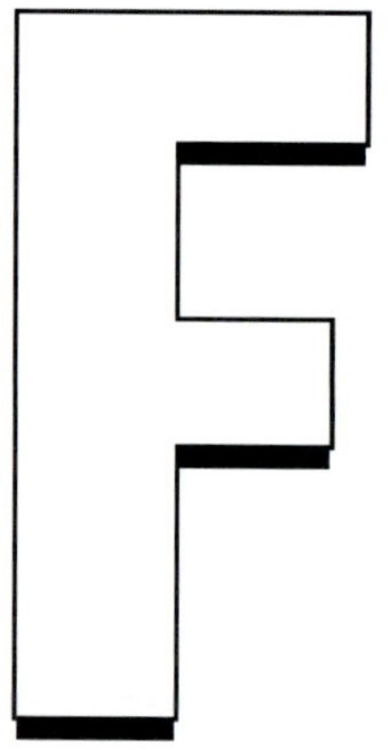

FROM THE START THEY SEEMED LIKE UNLIKELY partners: the forthright, unfailingly moral Captain America and the seasoned, potentially lethal agent known as Black Widow. But through years of adventures together, as Widow sought to wipe out the red in her ledger and Cap became a little savvier about navigating the various political complexities of the modern world, Chris Evans's Steve Rogers and Scarlett Johansson's Natasha Romanoff have developed more than a healthy respect for each other—they've become close friends and allies, maybe even family.

Good thing too, since heading into *Avengers: Infinity War,* they'll need to be able to lean on each other for support. As Earth's mightiest heroes take on the mad titan Thanos (Josh Brolin), victory isn't necessarily assured, and not every Avenger is guaranteed to make it out alive. With the fate of the Marvel Cinematic Universe hanging in the balance, *EW* caught up with the longtime costars and friends—*Infinity War* and its as-yet-untitled 2019 follow-up will mark the actors' seventh and eighth screen collaboration since 2004's teen-heist movie *The Perfect Score*—to talk about the bond between their comic-book alter egos and whether their time in the superhero game might finally be nearing an end.

"I'm kind of nervous about it," Johansson says of the future, "but I'm also excited to have the opportunity to do something to give the character [closure]." *—Gina McIntyre (Reporting and interview by Anthony Breznican)*

Cap and Widow are together once again. Where do we find them at the beginning of this film?

CHRIS EVANS I think our values and morals align, and I think we both had some ups and downs when it came to working under a certain structure. I think we're answering to nobody.

SCARLETT JOHANSSON Which is how it has to be done, since there seems to be nobody really that we can trust. There's no greater organization really. It's all fallen apart. Nothing really makes sense, and everything's turned on its head....When you see us in [*Captain America: The Winter Soldier*] fighting this terrorist organization, we're doing that kind of work when you find us.

They're two heroes, two people with opposing points of view, but each of them is right.

SJ I think they see a like-mindedness that keeps them together. They have a friendship obviously. [That shared experience] is the basis of that. They're also unexpectedly in a similar situation in their lives.

CE They both experienced a disruption of a belief system. I think what's left is the only thing you can trust, a friendship.

Is Natasha feeling more confident? Is she lost? Steve seems to still be reeling in this perspective change, but Natasha is a little worldlier than he is.

SJ It's been a dark time. I wouldn't say necessarily that my character has been particularly hopeful, but I think she's hardened even more than she probably was before. Going rogue and living underground for a couple years, that does something to you, and the fact that it's a thankless task what you're doing is a heavy burden that you carry....I'm still trying to figure it out exactly. This film is so plot-driven that unfortunately we don't have so much space for character work, but I assume that, not to say exactly that she's unraveled a little bit, but I think the thrill she gets is from relief, like fighting and going into battle. I imagine there's a little bit of a nihilistic quality to her at this

STEVE'S A BIT MORE HARDENED NOW.... HE'S SEEN MORE, HE'S LEARNED MORE"

—CHRIS EVANS

A newly bearded Steve Rogers (Chris Evans) is ready to pick up Captain America's shield once more.

point. I'm going in that direction. We'll see how it lands.

CE It's always felt like Natasha uses her cynicism as a defense mechanism. She weaponizes it for survival. I think Steve is a little newly calloused in the ways of the world, and I think from the birth of their friendship it's always felt that Natasha looks out for Steve in a way. There's a little bit of naïveté to him, and I think she nurtures that.

That's still there?

CE Well, I still think they have a bond as a result of it. I think Steve's a bit more hardened now because he's seen more, he's learned more. Natasha is always going to be a couple steps ahead of him in terms of experience and knowledge. They've leaned on each other for different reasons. It's reinforced the friendship.

Steve has a huge chunk of his life that's just missing. Is that still weighing on him? Or has he moved on at this point?

CE I think getting Bucky (Sebastian Stan) back was a really nice piece of the puzzle. When you break up with someone, you're heartbroken until you get your new girlfriend. I think his creating a new family, creating new roots or identifying with a new understanding of what home is, I think has helped him cope with what he's lost. There's always a piece of that in him. I think that's where he pulls his innocence from.

You take anything like *Star Wars* or Marvel, James Bond—actors play these parts for a long time, and then they move on. How do you think you'll look back on this time in your careers when you're not doing these movies anymore?

CE I think it's tough to process when you're in it. I think even the Mark Hamills and the Harrison Fords would say while they were doing it, it's tough to process what you're a part of until later. We've been doing this for so long now. It's tough to step back and see the painting you're making. It's nice to know that it's having an impact. It's nice to know that it's certainly pioneering in a way, in terms of this web of multiple universes. But I don't know if I can exactly say what it means to me or how I'm processing it, because being part of it makes it hard to get the real flavor.

Do you feel like you're reaching the end of an arc for your characters?

SJ It's been now eight years or so that I've been developing this character; I'd like to see the arc come full circle. I think that would be satisfying. I want to be able to really feel a sense of accomplishment, and I don't think I would have that if it was just so open-ended.

It's a bittersweet thing obviously. It's a character that I love to play. Not only do we also have a really great film family here, but it's also a character that I feel very close to because I've grown with [her]. So many things have happened in my life as I played this character. It's kind of bittersweet to imagine that the arc will have some end. I think it'll be necessary. It has to have a resolution.

WIDOW GOES SOLO?

The only female Avenger might—finally—be striking out on her own with a new big-screen adventure. **BY SEAN SMITH**

It's the question that Marvel fans have been asking for years: When is Black Widow getting her own movie? It looks like the time might finally be at hand. Marvel, reportedly in consultation with Scarlett Johansson, has hired Jac Schaeffer to write the script. (Schaeffer's own star has been on the rise thanks to a hot screenplay titled *The Shower,* about a baby shower interrupted by an alien invasion.) No director has been hired yet, and no start date has been set. In the meantime, Marvel will release its first female-led superhero solo film next March with *Captain Marvel,* starring Oscar winner Brie Larson (Room). Talk is swirling too about a possible all-female team-up of Marvel heroines that could include not only Widow but also Tessa Thompson's Valkyrie, Zoe Saldana's Gamora and more. Can't wait.

SHIELD OF DREAMS

Captain America might have a new shield thanks to Wakandan technology, but the original will never go out of style. **BY GLENN GREENBERG**

Forget Bucky and the Falcon. Captain America's real partner is his shield, which he's had since 1943.

Created by inventor-industrialist Howard Stark for Cap during World War II, the shield is made of vibranium, the ultrarare metal found in the Black Panther's African homeland of Wakanda. It has protected Steve Rogers (Chris Evans) from everything that's ever been aimed at him—bullets, explosions, alien death rays, even Thor's hammer. The shield is also a highly effective projectile. With one skillfully executed throw, it can take out Rogers's adversaries, ricochet and return to his waiting hand.

While Cap himself has gotten several makeovers since he emerged from the ice where he'd been frozen for nearly 70 years, his shield has stayed almost exactly the same. "With Cap, the shield has to work with the costume," says *Avengers: Infinity War* costume designer Judianna Makovsky, who also worked on *Captain America: The Winter Soldier* (2014) and *Captain America: Civil War* (2016). "Overall it doesn't change that much, since it's based on the one in the comic. But in *Civil War* it became darker, more scratched, and the colors were a little different. A lot of that comes from the sensibilities of [directors Anthony and Joe Russo], who wanted to make everything more real and not so bright and 'poppy.'"

Scarred in *Civil War* during a battle between Cap and Black Panther, the shield was last seen in the possession of Tony Stark (Robert Downey Jr.), with Steve Rogers having apparently abandoned his superhero identity. But there's no way Rogers will be without a shield for very long—even if he has to go all the way to Wakanda to get it.

PHOTOGRAPH BY JUSTIN FANTL

•WINTER SOLDIER *Sebastian Stan*

TO BORROW A PHRASE FROM BLACK WIDOW, Bucky Barnes (Sebastian Stan) has got an awful lot of red in his ledger.

Barnes grew up as the childhood best friend of Steve Rogers (Chris Evans), and both served together in World War II. But after being captured by HYDRA, he eventually transformed into a weapon of mass destruction. Over the years he's shot Black Widow (Scarlett Johansson) through the stomach and left her for dead, staged an attempt on the life of Nick Fury (Samuel L. Jackson) and was then framed for the terrorist bombing that kills the father of Black Panther (Chadwick Boseman) in 2016's *Captain America: Civil War.*

And all of that was before the Avengers learned that he was the man who murdered Tony Stark's (Robert Downey Jr.) parents, a secret that threatens to permanently sever Cap and Iron Man's alliance. "He himself doesn't really know who he is," Stan told *EW* in 2016. "He signed up to go to war and do the right thing for his country and ended up becoming a brainwashed Manchurian Candidate assassin." Throughout it all, his lifelong pal Rogers has steadfastly believed that the Winter Solider programming can be reversed. But Barnes himself remains soul-sick with guilt. "What you did all those years...it wasn't you," Cap tells him in *Civil War.* Barnes replies, "I know. But I did it."

Now, after a deprogramming trip to Wakanda, Barnes appears ready to begin his recovery. If the Avengers can forgive him—and if he can forgive himself—the newly rechristened White Wolf will be an invaluable weapon in the coming *Infinity War.* —*Sean Smith*

SCARLET WITCH

Elizabeth Olsen

FEW AVENGERS HAVE SUFFERED MORE sorrow than Wanda Maximoff (Elizabeth Olsen). She and her twin brother, Pietro (Aaron Taylor-Johnson), were orphaned at age 10 and underwent HYDRA experiments that gave them powers courtesy of the Mind Stone. In 2015's *Avengers: Age of Ultron,* they join with Ultron, but when the villain's designs are uncovered, the twins switch sides. Pietro dies in the battle, devastating Wanda.

She soon forms an enduring bond with Vision (Paul Bettany), and at the end of *Civil War* they escape to Europe. But their domestic bliss is threatened by Thanos's plans. "She keeps attaching herself to things that fulfill her world, and they keep going away," says Olsen. She may be unprepared for another loss. —*S.S. (additional reporting by Anthony Breznican)*

FALCON

Anthony Mackie

HE'S THE ULTIMATE WINGMAN. SAM WILSON (ANTHONY MACKIE) HAS been Captain America's fiercest ally since the two former military men met on a morning run in *Captain America: The Winter Soldier.* They may be generations apart, but their joint sense of patriotism and morality has formed the bedrock of their friendship.

After Wilson provided a safe house to Cap and Black Widow as they hid from undercover HYDRA forces, he volunteered to join them in their mission—and he's had Steve Rogers's back ever since. At the end of *Civil War,* Falcon is captured and Rogers escapes. Now, as *Avengers: Infinity War* begins, Falcon has gone underground. "He can't just go back to his regular life, because he's a marked man," Mackie told *EW* on-set. When Cap needs him again, Falcon will be there. —*S.S. (additional reporting by Anthony Breznican)*

ANT-MAN *Paul Rudd*

WHEN THE WORLD NEEDS A HERO WHO LOOKS out for the little guy, it helps to be the little guy. Scott Lang (Paul Rudd) is Marvel's tiniest titan of justice. An ex-con with a Robin Hood ethos, Lang is an electrical engineer who uses his wit, intelligence and training—and a suit that shrinks him to the size of an insect—to take down the corrupt and powerful. But his real motivation is more intimate. Lang initially agrees to become Ant-Man for the sole purpose of getting enough money to pay back child support and regain visitation rights to see his young daughter Cassie. "He's not used to being a hero," *Ant-Man* director Peyton Reed told *EW* before the release of that 2015 film. "He's more like George Clooney in *Ocean's Eleven*. He's a guy trying to create a new life for himself and find redemption."

Aided by the first Ant-Man, Dr. Hank Pym (Michael Douglas), and trained by Pym's ambitious (and crushworthy) daughter Hope Van Dyne (Evangeline Lilly), Lang attracts the attention of the Avengers when he defeats Falcon (Anthony Mackie) by shrinking and disabling Falcon's suit. When the lines are drawn for *Civil War,* Lang cheerfully joins Team Captain America, turning in a surprise appearance as Giant-Man to help Steve Rogers (Chris Evans). Now, as the Avengers join forces again in April's *Infinity War,* Lang will need to adapt, but he's proved he can be pretty helpful at any size. Best of all, we know he survives. *Ant-Man and the Wasp,* which sees Lilly donning some pretty cool armor of her own, arrives three months after *Infinity War.* Two movies in three months? That's big. —*S.S.*

▲
Left: Paul Rudd as Ant-Man. Right: Rudd and Evangeline Lilly suit up for *Ant-Man and the Wasp*.

◀
Rudd and Lilly train together in 2015's *Ant-Man*.

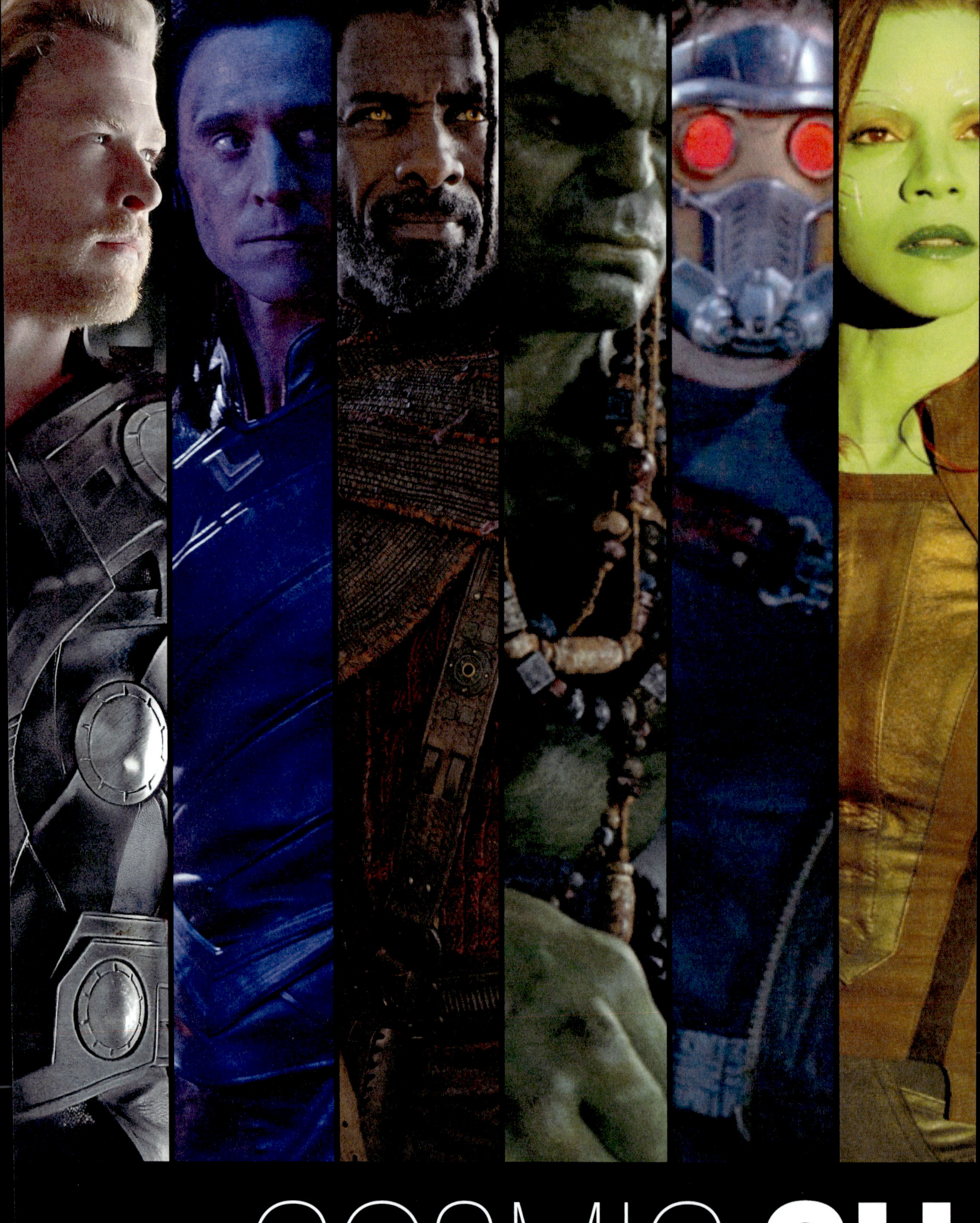

COSMIC **SU**

PER HEROES

GOD OF *WAR*

WHO NEEDS A HAMMER ANYWAY? THE HILARIOUS (AND WAY-OUT-THERE) *THOR: RAGNAROK* MARKED THE THIRD SOLO OUTING FOR THE POWERFUL ASGARDIAN, AND ITS MANY WILD TWISTS DRIVE THE GOD'S ROLE IN *AVENGERS: INFINITY WAR*

The mid-credits scene of *Thor: Ragnarok* teased the arrival of Thanos's ship—and things didn't appear to go smoothly for Chris Hemsworth's Thor in the trailer for *Avengers: Infinity War*.

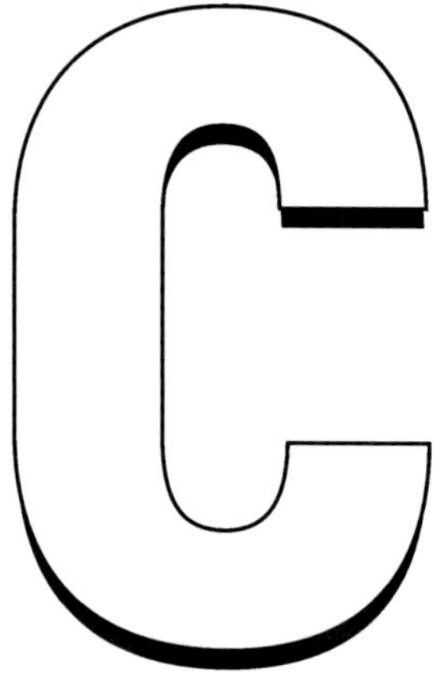

CHRIS HEMSWORTH'S HERO HAS COME A long way since 2011's *Thor,* during which he initially lost his hammer, met love-interest Jane Foster (Natalie Portman) and was betrayed by adopted brother Loki (Tom Hiddleston) for the first of many times. Since then, the good-natured god of thunder joined the Avengers, dragged Loki back to Asgard in chains, then saw his home world destroyed—twice. In *Thor: The Dark World* he mourned his mother, Frigga (Rene Russo); in *Thor: Ragnarok* he said farewell to pops Odin (Anthony Hopkins) and then was forced to immediately defend Asgard against his older sister Hela, the vampy goddess of death (Cate Blanchett). In 2017 *EW*'s Anthony Breznican sat down with Hemsworth on the set of *Avengers: Infinity War.*

Thor is a little worse for wear by the time he turns up in *Infinity War.*

He has quite a physical transformation in a couple of ways—obviously the hair, his costume gets beat to hell and changed and altered, as does his attitude, I think. He now is in a world where he's no longer privileged, special or any more powerful than the majority of people he's up against. I think some of my favorite parts in the Thor journey over the years is the first film, when he lost his powers, because an audience can sort of empathize with him in that sense or relate to him. It's also a great journey to try and gather back your power or try to earn that power.

What's his mind-set at the start?

He's softened quite a great deal. This feels very personal to him as opposed to some sort of responsibility to the team or to the Avengers.

Thor spends some time with a couple of Guardians, specifically Groot and Rocket. What's the personality cocktail like there?

That's been a hell of a lot of fun. Each time you interact with somebody different, they bring out a different element in that character, and it was quite a strange, quirky dynamic between the three of them. It ended up being a road trip, kind of a buddy-cop quest, in a way, and quite the odd pairing. [Thor] has a great deal of respect for Rocket, which is a little misdirected. But Rocket thinks, "Fantastic! Someone's finally paying me some respect." Then obviously Groot tags along with Rocket.

And Thor's perspective on Groot? Just another tall, silent type?

Yeah, he doesn't have any strange judgment. I think Thor, he's seen all sorts of creatures and is used to the oddness of it all and the quirkiness. I guess because of maybe [*Thor: Ragnarok*] as well, not much can surprise him at this point.

Ragnarok looked like fun.

I really wanted to do something different. I'd sort of become really bored with myself as that character and wanted to do something else with it. It felt fresh and it was a little more offbeat, the humor. It started with the writing, who was directing. [Filmmaker Taika Waititi] was certainly a vastly different choice than what you would have thought for that character. [There was] a whole lot of improvisation. It was great. It was quite liberating in that sense. . . . In fact I said that to Taika the other day about the director's cut, and he goes, "It's going to be about four hours long. It's going to be every wacky improvised thing we did."

Thor and Cap have, I think, one of the most interesting moments in this whole series of films. It's kind of a throwaway, but it's really important: when they're trying to move the hammer in the *Age of Ultron*, and Thor's just like, "Good luck, everybody." He's kind of smirking, and then Cap kind of budges it a little bit . . .

I would like so much more time to explore that sort of stuff. . . . To this day [that] is the scene that people say is their favorite scene. It's relatable. It's human. People like to see these characters step outside of their heroic stature and be regular people. And I would love to have more scenes like that.

What's the personality like for Thanos? If he weren't a purple space villain, what kind of guy would he be on Earth?

Probably Al Capone-esque but far more physically imposing and brutal. He's not relying just on his henchmen to do the dirty work. He's dishing it out himself. He's kind of mafioso-esque.

Those guys have to be sort of political. They're charismatic. They have to lead people.

He's quite [committed to] keeping order and maintaining some sort of structure to things, however brutal his task may be. Now look, I'm not the most educated on Al Capone, but I just mean, that sort of persona I've seen in movies, where there is a charisma and you find yourself enjoying watching him roll through chaos. Then you go, "God, I'm not rooting for the bad guy here, am I?" But I think that's because of what Josh [Brolin] brings to it and the writing that they've given him to play with.

You only saw the script pages for your part in the film.

They offered me the chance to read the script, and by the time that chance was presented, I was like, well, we're already shooting now. I thought, I'll wait to see the movie to find out what's going on. But I knew my journey, and I think that's all you need to know. And I really liked Thor's journey in this, and so it makes the premiere all the more exciting.

HAMMER TIME

Thor's got a brand-new weapon to wield in *Avengers: Infinity War*, but the mystical Mjolnir will always be close to the thunder god's heart. **BY GLENN GREENBERG**

It might be gone, but the mighty Mjolnir is hardly forgotten. The hammer bestowed upon Chris Hemsworth's thunder god by his father, Odin (Anthony Hopkins), was "forged in the heart of a dying star.... Its power has no equal—as a weapon, to destroy, or as a tool, to build." Through Mjolnir, Thor could summon and project lightning. He could use the hammer to propel himself through the air, to deflect energy blasts and to act as a controlled projectile that returns to him. As such, it had to look like a mythic artifact, not something you'd find at the local hardware store.

"It needed to be exquisite, it needed to look valuable and it needed to appear to be extraordinarily heavy," says Charles Wood, who served as production designer on 2013's *Thor: The Dark World*, 2015's *Avengers: Age of Ultron* and 2018's *Avengers: Infinity War*. "We needed to make sure we built a prop that actually felt like only a god could pick it up, and that's quite a challenge."

Early in *Thor* (2011), Odin banishes his son from Asgard because of his arrogance and recklessness. He also places a spell on Mjolnir, declaring, "Whosoever holds this hammer, if he be worthy, shall possess the power of Thor"—meaning no hammer for Hemsworth's hero until he proves himself worthy again. (As we know from *Age of Ultron*, Chris Evans's Captain America can move Mjolnir, ever so slightly, while Paul Bettany's Vision can lift it with ease.)

Unfortunately Thor and Mjolnir's bond was broken again—seemingly forever—when Hela, the goddess of death (Cate Blanchett), turns up in *Thor: Ragnarok* (2017) and destroys the hammer. But Thor eventually realizes that he has plenty of power all by his lonesome. He's not the god of hammers after all.

PHOTOGRAPH BY JUSTIN FANTL

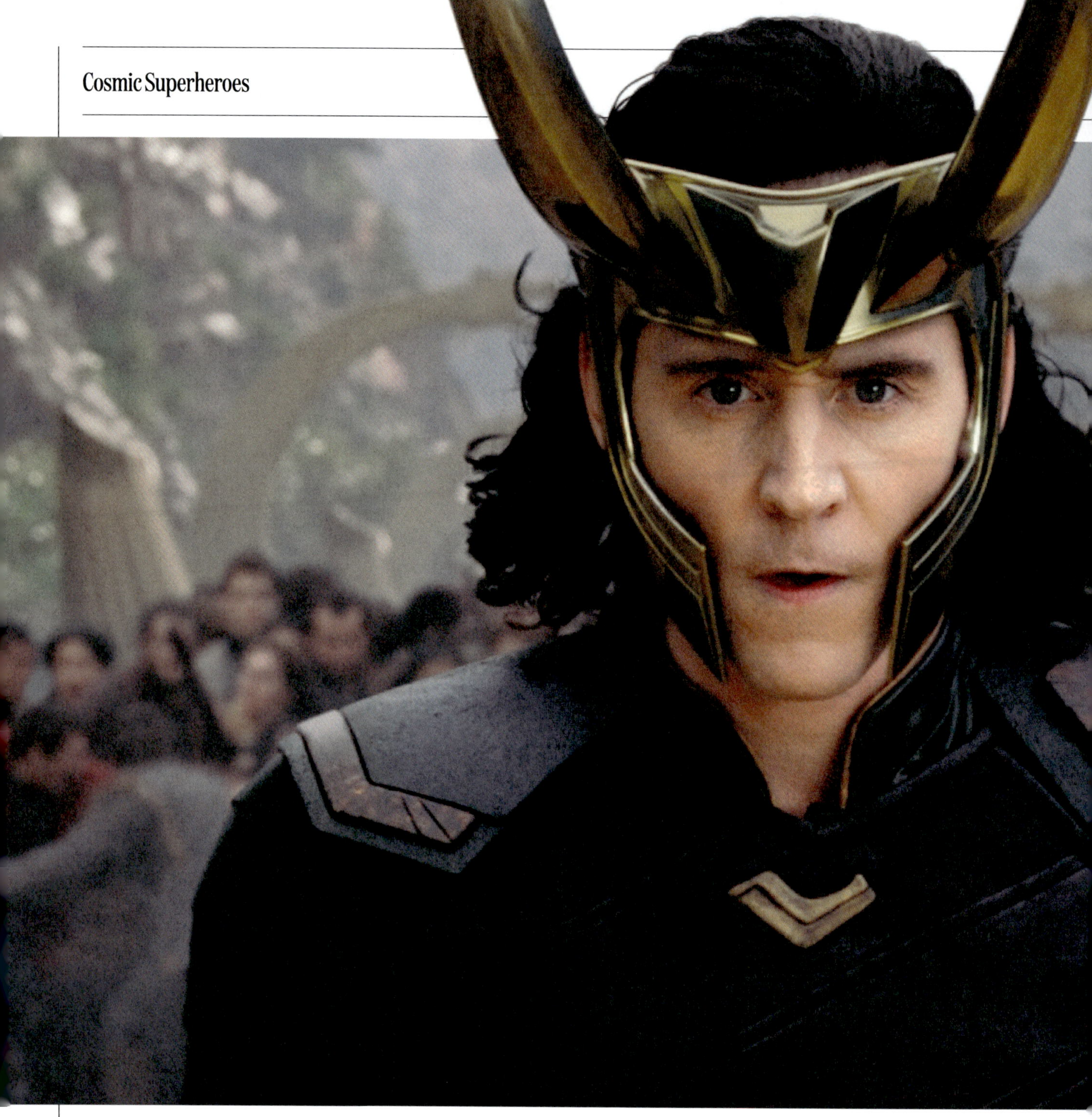

LOKI *Tom Hiddleston*

TOM HIDDLESTON'S TRICKSTER GOD OF THE Marvel Cinematic Universe has been on a (way) circuitous route toward demi-heroism over the course of four films. Will he find final redemption in *Avengers: Infinity War* or orchestrate his final act of betrayal?

Loki may be the most relatable—and charismatic—villain in superhero lore. Loki grew up feeling that he drew the short straw against the golden-tressed charms of his brother Thor (Chris Hemsworth), heir to the Asgard throne. Pale, raven-haired and smart, Loki represents the brainy goth sibling of every high school football-team captain or head cheerleader. He is not the chosen one, and he resents the hell out of it. "We were raised together," Thor pleads with Loki in *The Avengers*. "We played together. We fought together. Do you remember none of that?" He does, but not quite that way. "I remember a shadow," Loki replies, "living in the shade of your greatness."

During his time in the MCU, Loki has discovered that he was adopted and that his biological father was the king of the Frost Giants. He has secretly launched a war against his own people, seized the throne, kept his brother in exile, been imprisoned, faked his own death, impersonated his father, Odin (Anthony Hopkins), mind-controlled Hawkeye (Jeremy Renner), formed a pact with Thanos (Josh Brolin) that would give Loki dominion over Earth and generally been the sharpest thorn in Thor's side. But when we last saw him in *Thor: Ragnarok,* he had managed to slightly redeem himself—naturally, after an attempt at betrayal—by helping his bro destroy their sister Hela (Cate Blanchett) and transport the surviving population of their planet to ours. Once again the trickster proves that whatever you expect from Loki will not be what you get. —***Sean Smith***

HEIMDALL

Idris Elba

HE SEES AND HEARS ALL. THE ASGARDIAN gatekeeper and amber-eyed guardian of the Bifrost bridge is the omniscient observer of everything that happens in Marvel's nine realms. But he is no passive oracle dispensing wisdom from on high. Heimdall (Idris Elba) is a warrior.

Loyal to the people of Asgard above all else, he has remained devoted to Thor, battled Loki, crossed Thor's father, Odin, confessed to treason and been exiled—all in service to his planet. For Elba the role has been satisfying, though he'd welcome the opportunity to play a bigger part. "I wish I was more present in the Marvel family," he told *EW* last fall. "It's been great, but I kind of think I need a bit more. I want to be a superhero. I like the idea of that."

In *Thor: Ragnarok,* Heimdall certainly had plenty of heroic screen time, fending off Hela and creating a secret refuge for the Asgardians before later attempting to ferry them across the bridge to Earth. He fought valiantly alongside Thor, Hulk (Mark Ruffalo) and Valkyrie (Tessa Thompson). Now, with Asgard itself destroyed, his future is unclear. But there's no doubt that he will defend his people at all costs. —***S.S.***

HULK *Mark Ruffalo*

NO AVENGER HAS DARKER DEMONS THAN Bruce Banner—unlike almost every other superhero, his rageaholic alter ego Hulk is outside his control. That internal struggle has made Banner Marvel's most reluctant of heroes. He's a man of science and intellect consumed and subsumed by his own emotions. He's a comic-book hero by way of Freud or Shakespeare.

"They're splitting," actor Mark Ruffalo says of the two sides of his character. "They're both struggling for primacy. Banner's able to stay Banner longer, and Hulk is able to stay Hulk longer. They're becoming more defined, and the struggle between them is becoming more and more accentuated."

When last we saw him in *Thor: Ragnarok*, the brilliant scientific mind had been bottled up for two years while Hulk had taken command and had been living as a gladiator god (with his own swanky apartment, no less) on the faraway planet of Sakaar. "Banner hates Hulk," Ruffalo says. "He really resents him, and Hulk really resents Banner. There's so much bad blood between them, and [in *Ragnarok*] they both express it."

Of course Banner eventually reemerges and helps Thor (Chris Hemsworth) defeat Hela (Cate Blanchett), but two years off Earth—and in the Marvel equivalent of the phantom zone—has taken a toll on him as *Avengers: Infinity War* begins. When he returns to Earth, his mission is to find the Avengers and warn them of Thanos's plan. "Basically he's playing the chorus," Ruffalo says. "He lays a lot of expositional groundwork for a lot of the story. He's jumping between different groups a lot. He starts off with Thor, and then he ends up with Iron Man."

But could he also maybe end up with Black Widow? The romance between Banner and Scarlett Johansson's Natasha Romanoff has been simmering for years now. Assuming the heroes can thwart Thanos and save the galaxy, could that lay out a pathway for the scientist and the spy to (finally!) end up together? Only one thing's for sure, Ruffalo says of Banner's future: "None of the old rules apply." —***Sean Smith** (**additional reporting by Anthony Breznican**)*

SPACE CADETS

THE BAND OF BANTER-HAPPY MISFITS GANG UP, BREAK OUT OF PRISON AND THEN SET ASIDE THEIR DIFFERENCES TO STOP ONE OF THANOS' AGENTS FROM CLAIMING AN INFINITY STONE. THEY'VE BEEN TOGETHER, MOSTLY, EVER SINCE. *By Sean Smith (Additional reporting by Anthony Breznican)*

The Guardians of the Galaxy will join the greater world of the Marvel Cinematic Universe in *Avengers: Infinity War.* From left: Star-Lord (Chris Pratt), Groot (Vin Diesel), Gamora (Zoe Saldana), Mantis (Pom Klementieff), Rocket (Bradley Cooper) and Drax (Dave Bautista).

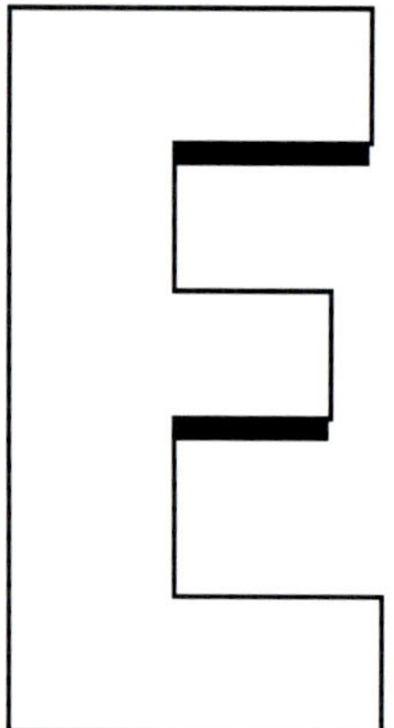

EVER SINCE INTERGALACTIC MERCENARY Peter Quill/Star-Lord and his not-so-merry band of outlaws jacked up the Marvel universe with their middle-finger morality, horn-dog innuendo and skin-of-their-teeth heroism, fans have been dreaming of the day these smart-ass scofflaws would crash the Avengers' oh-so-earnest party. The wait is over.

In *Avengers: Infinity War,* Quill (Chris Pratt), Gamora (Zoe Saldana), Rocket (Bradley Cooper), Groot (Vin Diesel), Drax (Dave Bautista)—and Drax's new antennaed crush, Mantis (Pom Klementieff)—bring their magic space dust to the epic fight with the evil Thanos for the fate of, uh, everything. For Gamora and her sister Nebula (Karen Gillan), the battle is especially personal—given that its their adoptive father the once-enemies, now-allies are facing. Dad should watch his back. "Because Thanos is the villain, his daughters are involved in that whole situation," Saldana says. "It was so much fun."

Whether the Avengers will find Quill and squad "fun" is a bit of a question mark—it's kinda difficult to picture Pratt's goofy Star-Lord kicking back with Chris Evans's by-the-book Captain America. When Thor (Chris Hemsworth) spies the group, he seems more confused. "Who the hell are you guys?" he asks.

It's not a bad question—and it's one the Guardians are wrestling with themselves. After saving Xandar from genocidal Ronan (Lee Pace) in the first film, they became the rock-star saviors of the galaxy, only to fall from their perch in the second installment. Their ragtag family faced some shaky internal tsuris, what with Star-Lord desperate to find a father figure in Kurt Russell's cruel Ego and Rocket (Bradley Cooper) inviting the enmity of the Sovereign and their leader Ayesha (Elizabeth Debicki) by stealing their prized Anulax batteries.

At the same time, Peter and Gamora's mutual attraction seems to be heating up, and Drax (Dave Bautista) and Mantis (Pom Klementieff) appear to be on the cusp of becoming the cutest odd couple in all of space-time. And adorable Baby Groot (Vin Diesel)? He's now a surly adolescent. (Brace yourself for the inevitable "sprouting wood" jokes.)

Much is riding on the Guardians' future. Once this phase of Marvel's Cinematic Universe concludes with Avengers 4 in 2019, the characters' next solo adventure will help shape everything that follows. "[*Guardians of the Galaxy Vol. 3*] will take place after the next two Avengers movies, and it will help to set up the next 10, 20 years of Marvel movies," writer-director James Gunn told *EW* in 2017. "It's going to really expand the cosmic universe."

That's pretty poetic redemption for the group of "a--holes" who were never the most recognizable of Marvel's trove of superheroes. Before *Guardians of the Galaxy* was released in 2014, fans and critics both wondered whether the film would become the studio's first miss in an unbroken string of hits. Instead it grossed almost $800 million worldwide, blasted Pratt onto the A-list and set a new creative direction for Marvel.

The movie's cheeky, absurdist tone injected a jet stream of joy into a genre dominated by the sinister, serious approach of DC's Dark Knight films and the earnestness of Marvel's own Avengers. Since then we've seen Guardians' nimble action-comedy alchemy launch Ant-Man, resurrect Spider-Man, rejuvenate Thor and even power the kinky, hard-R stylings of a Marvel character not directly under the studio's purview: Deadpool.

Unburdened from the need to make a larger point about higher values or the socio-political state of the world, the Guardians made superheroism seem like fun again. And no one understands that better than the Star-Lord. "I love my character, and I love this world," Pratt told *EW* in 2018. "There are a lot more stories to tell."

▲ The Guardians line up in *Vol. 1* after causing a disturbance on the world of Xandar.

◀ Nebula has a complicated relationship with pop Thanos and fellow adopted sibling Camora. At the end of *Vol. 2*, she had vowed to bring down the mad titan.

•DOCTOR STRANGE *Benedict Cumberbatch*

TRUTH BE TOLD, DR. STEPHEN VINCENT Strange (Benedict Cumberbatch) was a superhero in his own head long before he actually became one. The world's most gifted neurosurgeon, blessed with a photographic memory, believed himself a medical god. "Strange is incredibly arrogant, brilliant, sort of extraordinary," Cumberbatch said, before the character's debut in 2016's *Doctor Strange*. "And his need to control fates, to control destiny and, in particular, death, has brought him to the height of his profession."

When a life-threatening car accident shatters Strange's hands beyond repair, he goes to any lengths to find a cure. When all medical options are exhausted, he travels to Nepal hoping for an answer from the mystical realm. But it's not until the Ancient One (Tilda Swinton) gives the skeptic a little inter-dimensional wake-up call that he starts to appreciate the powers of the cosmos. Believing finally that his life can have meaning again, Strange surrenders his old life to become a Master of the Mystic Arts.

The Sorcerer Supreme is only drafted into service when the stakes are crazy high. "We've always assumed that the sorcerers have bigger fish to fry when they hear there's...a bank being robbed," Marvel Studios president Kevin Feige said in 2016. "They're thinking, 'If we don't keep vigilant, our sense of reality will disappear, and there won't be a bank to rob and there won't be a city to be conquered.'" In terms of *Infinity War*, expect Strange to break out a few metaphysical party tricks before the last dance. *—Sean Smith*

THE EYE HAS IT

An ancient relic worn by Doctor Strange, the Eye of Agamotto contains the Time Stone, one of the powerful infinity gems coveted by the mad titan Thanos. **BY CLARK COLLIS**

Time waits for no man. The Sorcerer Supreme on the other hand? That's another story. "The Eye of Agamotto can manipulate probabilities, which is another way of saying 'screw around with time,'" Marvel Studios president Kevin Feige told *EW* in 2016.

The powerful Nepalese-inspired amulet made its debut in 2016's *Doctor Strange,* when Benedict Cumberbatch's character trapped the evil being Dormammu in a time loop using the mystical artifact. Its design, surprisingly, "wasn't that difficult," according to *Doctor Strange* director Scott Derrickson. "It was so cool—we knew we didn't have to improve greatly upon what was in the comics for it to be interesting for a modern audience."

But wearing the Eye came with its challenges for Cumberbatch, says *Avengers: Infinity War* prop master Russell Bobbitt: "It bothered him if it swung as it hung, so we made a magnetic version that clung to his body." These days Strange is rarely seen without the Eye, but he's far from dependent on the object for his powers—the guy's blessed with an abracadabra arsenal that could make even Loki jealous. Good thing too, since Thanos (Josh Brolin) is sure to try to claim the Time Stone for his gauntlet.

"[Strange] has a Cloak of Levitation that allows him to fly," Feige says. "He can create mandalas of light as shields and whips. He can create portals to go to other places around the world." Strange indeed. *(additional reporting by Chancellor Agard and Piya Sinha-Roy)*

THE WORLD o

f WAKANDA

ALL HAIL T'CHALLA

***BLACK PANTHER* STAR CHADWICK BOSEMAN BROKE BARRIERS AND BOX OFFICE RECORDS IN HIS HISTORY-MAKING FIRST SOLO OUTING AS THE KING OF WAKANDA. FOR *AVENGERS: INFINITY WAR*, HE'S BACK—AND BETTER THAN EVER.** *By Anthony Breznican*

The King returns! Black Panther (Chadwick Boseman) prepares for war.

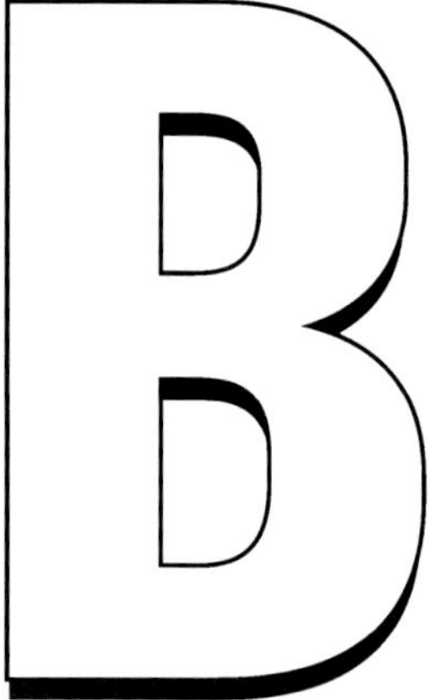

BLACK PANTHER DOESN'T SMILE. WHEN HE bares his teeth, it usually means someone's about to get hurled through a wall or against a car. And that snarl is always hidden beneath his obsidian-hued mask. T'Challa certainly has charisma, but the former prince—now king—of Wakanda is not a wisecracking kind of hero. As the ruler of that fictional African kingdom, he's got the weight of a whole nation on his shoulders, so there's a gravity to the man that Chadwick Boseman (*42*, *Get on Up*) is bringing to life. Wakanda is not welcoming to outsiders, and Marvel fans have been waiting a long time to visit, especially after a brief glimpse of the exotic locale at the end of *Captain America: Civil War*. With the February release of *Black Panther*, that border finally opened—and with it an overdue cinematic breakthrough for people of color.

But when Wakanda opened up its doors, trouble stepped through. In *Avengers: Infinity War* the technologically advanced nation becomes a battleground to save the universe. That's good for the planet (and other denizens of the galaxy) but not so good for Wakandans. Boseman says Wakanda will serve another purpose too: It becomes the key to synching up the disparate aspects of the MCU. "Each movie has a different style, you know?" the actor says. "So what is a Captain America movie versus an Iron Man movie versus the Black Panther movie, and how do you bring those things together? They're different voices. So how do those voices harmonize?"

Looks like we're all about to find out.

What's T'Challa's place in the world at the point that *Infinity War* begins?
At the start of *Black Panther*, obviously my father [T'Chaka, played by John Kani] has been killed. So with the death of a leader there's always an opening where someone can come in and take over, and there will be factions that will support that. So that's definitely a carry-over into this movie. I think what's important is that he's developed the relationship from *Civil War* with Cap (Chris Evans) in order to participate in the battles of this movie. They trust each other.

Why do you think that is?
He spent time in Wakanda. He participated in both sides of the argument, in terms of superheroes registering what his place in the world is. I think it has to do with that.

This is the first time Wakanda's been invaded, right? When Thanos comes in?
Wakanda's history...expands beyond recorded history. But it has not been conquered. They've definitely been challenged.

This movie has a certain gravity. It's the culmination of the whole Marvel Cinematic Universe for the last 10 years.
Reading the script I feel that. I can't feel the whole 10 years because I haven't been around for the whole 10 years....But it's amazing to read a script that involves so many different elements. And there's always a challenge in doing a movie, and

part of it is you have to pull a little bit from [each film]. I've watched those movies, and I [see] that harmony in the script and also in the way it's being directed at certain times. Whether it's a light moment, a serious moment, whether it's ritualistic or whatever—it's all being harmonized.

The screenwriters Christopher Markus and Stephen McFeely were saying they like to create odd couples, characters who don't get along. Is there a character that Panther has a particular grievance with? He's more like the host of the party, because it's his country.

Yeah, he's the host. So it's a little different, in terms of he doesn't have that clash with anyone, where the opposition of the characters automatically breeds conflict, which is basically what you're saying. That doesn't really exist here.

This is such a different dynamic than *Civil War*.

It's essentially like creating a whole bunch of buddy movies. *48 Hrs.* within [the Marvel universe]. So you've got Thor and Rocket together, those combinations. But with me, I don't really see that in this film.

You seem to spend quite a bit of time with Danai Gurira, who, of course, plays Okoye, the general of Wakanda's defense and head of the Dora Milaje secret service.

Yeah, I'm with my regular [crew]. And with the crew that I've built.

FIT FOR A KING

Fashioned from vibranium, T'Challa's one-of-a-kind suit is a sleek, fearsome weapon in its own right. BY GLENN GREENBERG

When Chadwick Boseman's T'Challa made his long-awaited big-screen debut in 2016's *Captain America: Civil War,* it was inside a bulletproof suit with retractable claws and a helmet woven with vibranium, the precious metal found in the kingdom of Wakanda. "That suit allowed him to get hit and fall, and the vibranium threads would absorb [or] negate the blunt force trauma, but that was kind of the extent of what it could do," says *Avengers: Infinity War* visual-effects supervisor Dan DeLeeuw.

Since then, you can bet that Black Panther's suit has gotten some serious upgrades—courtesy of T'Challa's brilliant inventor sister Shuri (Letitia Wright), sort of the Q to his James Bond. In *Black Panther* the outfit is sleeker with fewer prominent surface details. And when it comes to capabilities? Watch out. "It went from being what we had in *Civil War,* where it was just woven with vibranium threads, to being in and of itself a weapon," DeLeeuw says. "It has the ability to start from a small point and cover his body spontaneously." That includes T'Challa's head—the helmet, which was once a separate piece, is now incorporated into the rest of the suit. DeLeeuw says that the new outfit enables the hero to "absorb shocks and punches and redirect them against his enemies."

More upgrades lie ahead. "In *Infinity War,*" DeLeeuw says, "we take it to the next level."

BLACK PANTHER RULES THE WORLD

Audiences around the globe are embracing T'Challa as the undisputed new king of the superheroes—catapulting Marvel's massive hit to dizzying box office heights and widespread acclaim. **BY JEFF LABRECQUE**

"WHAT DO YOU KNOW ABOUT WAKANDA?" wily archvillain Ulysses Klaue (Andy Serkis) asks his CIA interrogator Everett Ross (Martin Freeman) in *Black Panther.* "Third-world backwater, textiles and shepherds," responds the bookish agent, reflecting the conventional wisdom about the reclusive African kingdom. A literal smokescreen, according to Klaue: In reality Wakanda is a futuristic paradise with wealth beyond our imagination.

For decades a similar conversation was going on in Hollywood about movies with black characters. They're niche films with limited box office, went the thinking. They're a risk because they won't play to an international audience. Such archaic arguments were already running on fumes, but then director Ryan Coogler pulled back the curtain and showed the world what it was missing. Weeks before *Black Panther* opened on Feb. 16, the most optimistic forecasts had predictions of a $100 million weekend. And then *Black Panther* delivered $202 million, the fifth-biggest opening weekend in history.

Critics paid homage too. Audiences, encouraged by positive word-of-mouth, fueled a mania, dressing as T'Challa (Chadwick Boseman), Okoye (Danai Gurira) or their other favorite Wakandan hero. "There's the moment in the movie where T'Challa, Okoye and Nakia (Lupita Nyong'o) are flying back to Wakanda for the first time, and he says, 'This never gets old...'" says Franklin Leonard, the founder of the influential Black List of hot Hollywood scripts. "I'm not going to lie—I got choked up. I was almost angry with myself for the inability to keep it together—but then I just sat back and let 13-year-old Franklin take over my brain, and I've never been quite so excited in a movie theater in my entire life."

On March 4 *Black Panther* crossed the $500 million mark faster than any film besides the last two episodic *Star Wars* installments, surging ahead of the pace set by *The Avengers* (2012), Marvel's biggest blockbuster to date. "The movie confirms a theory that I've had for over 20 years, which is a black sci-fi genre epic will transcend race," says Reginald Hudlin, who

▲ Left: Two cosplayers in Nairobi, Kenya, on Feb. 14, 2018. Right (from left): author Ta-Nehisi Coates with *Black Panther* stars Lupita Nyong'o and Chadwick Boseman.

directed Boseman in last year's *Marshall* and penned a *Black Panther* comic book for five years from 2006 to 2010. "*Black Panther* is the embodiment of every great thing about Africa—culturally, physically, morally, spiritually."

The film's appeal extends beyond any one demographic. "The inspirational and aspirational impact of this movie cannot be overstated," says Paul Dergarabedian, senior media analyst at comScore. "The international language of great superhero action applies to everybody, and there are universal themes—family, courage, redemption—that everyone can relate to."

Black Panther is a *Star Wars*-size phenomenon, but it's not an outlier either. The *Fast and the Furious* franchise demonstrated that an ethnically diverse cast (and director) was a force-multiplier; *Wonder Woman* cracked the glass ceiling for female superheroes and female directors. "The three fastest films to $500 million all have a black lead—and by the way, significant three-dimensional female parts," Leonard adds, referencing *Star Wars: The Force Awakens* and last year's *Star Wars: The Last Jedi*, featuring John Boyega as Finn.

Hudlin, who's set to direct a movie based on the *Shadowman* comic book, is already feeling the *Black Panther* Effect. "I've got studio executives calling me, like, 'Hey, you ready? We're ready!'" he says. "The audience has made it clear that they just want the cool thing. And if there's anything that black folks have been specialists in in 100 years of popular entertainment, it's that we deliver the cool thing." There's no going back.

HEAR US ROAR

ASIDE FROM BEING THE FIRST MARVEL STUDIOS FILM BUILT AROUND A PERSON OF COLOR, *BLACK PANTHER* FINALLY GIVES THE WOMEN THEIR DUE. LUPITA NYONG'O, DANAI GURIRA, ANGELA BASSETT AND LETITIA WRIGHT SAT DOWN WITH *EW* TO DISCUSS THEIR MOVIE AND WHAT IT MEANS FOR HOLLYWOOD'S FUTURE. *By Anthony Breznican*

Wright, Nyong'o, Bassett and Gurira photographed on Jan. 30, 2018, in Los Angeles.

WAKANDA HAS AT LEAST TWO PRECIOUS natural resources: a trove of the rare Vibranium mineral that has helped vault the secretive African nation a century (or more) ahead of the rest of the world—and valiant, fire-hearted females. Though Chadwick Boseman broke ground in *Black Panther* as Marvel Studios' first black leading man, the film also showcased an abundance of warrior women who all save the day in unique style. Emphasis on style. While Boseman's T'Challa must both protect and rule his kingdom, he depends a lot on the powerful women in his life. *The Walking Dead*'s Danai Gurira plays Okoye, the general in charge of Wakanda's defense and the head of the all-female Dora Milaje secret service, while Oscar winner Lupita Nyong'o steals the king's heart as Nakia, a Wakandan spy who's like James Bond and a Bond girl rolled into one. Meanwhile, T'Challa's brilliant little sis Shuri, played by Letitia Wright, is a Vibranium gadget master on par with Tony Stark, fashioning everything from Black Panther's kinetic armor to remote-control fighter jets. Finally, his newly widowed mother, Ramonda, played by Angela Bassett, brings the power of history to her son's throne.

We sat down with the women of Wakanda just a day after they first saw the finished film. They still seemed awestruck and praised director and cowriter Ryan Coogler (*Fruitvale Station, Creed*) for having their characters stand tall alongside the iconic male hero. Powerful women flanked Coogler as well, with cinematography by *Mudbound* Oscar nominee Rachel Morrison and dazzling costumes by Ruth E. Carter. "Watching the movie for the first time, I was seeing the different women occupy the same space and be their full selves, acting not with competition but with agency," Nyong'o says. "Their personal motivations are what lead them forward. They are not eye candy. Although..." She leans over to high-five the other women. "We do look pretty damn fly, I must say!"

What is it about the culture of Wakanda that creates such resilient, brilliant women?

ANGELA BASSETT It's a nation that respects and reveres women. They think of us not just as Queen but Queen Mother. Mother is nurturer and the first teacher. That position is embraced. She's not someone who is off to the side. Every mature woman is your auntie or your mother.

DANAI GURIRA And in contemporary African cultures, it's exactly that. It doesn't matter if she's a literal mother or not; an older woman is considered with respect. If you go into a store and you're greeting someone or calling out to someone, you call them "amai" in my country [she was born in Iowa but grew up in Zimbabwe]. That's something Wakanda brought to the forefront that was beautiful.

Is part of it also the lore of Wakanda? That this is a fictional place that has never been conquered, so it never had to adopt the outside world's views?

DG They were a nation uninterrupted.

▲ The all-female Dora Milaje is Wakanda's answer to the secret service.

They got to go through their full evolution. Other countries on the continent were very interrupted and traumatized through colonization. Wakanda didn't have that disruption. It was such an advanced nation, it actually allowed for evolution of gender roles. It recognized that you allow all your citizens to advance to their full potential.

LETITIA WRIGHT Wakanda as a nation is so open to forward movement. It will, hopefully, inspire us in reality to go, "Okay, cool, don't limit the women about what they want to do." [*Gestures to Nyong'o*] For example, Nakia is allowed to go out and be a spy and gather information for her nation, and she gets to choose whether she stays or goes. She's not controlled by anyone. That's powerful.

The same goes for your character, Shuri. She's trusted with creating the tools that keep her brother safe.

LW Her brother doesn't look down on her like, "Ugh, you're a kid, you can't make a suit for me." He's like, "No, this is your domain! Kill it!" Life for women in Wakanda is beautiful. It's inspirational. It's something I'm gonna take from watching this film in my own life and for the future of my children as well... [*laughs*] when I have a family.

LUPITA NYONG'O It was such a breath of fresh air seeing men and women living in their power without one dwarfing the other. To me it was reflective of the fact that sexism is learned. To see a society where that's not the focal point, where gender is not the fabric with which society

▲ Queen Ramonda (Bassett) stands at center, flanked by the Dora Milaje and daughter Shuri (Wright).

is built and the delineations of sex are not oppressive, that's cool.

That's the value of a story like this, right? It's an imaginary world, but it's nice to imagine things can be better. Why not?

DG Why not?! It really does make you say, "Why not?" To me, it's about equality and allowing each gender to come to the fullness of their potential without discriminatory hindrances. That is what this nation figured out.

Angela, what would you say makes Ramonda powerful? What makes her a hero?

AB She has the fine balance of mothering [T'Challa], of being there for him and being proud of him and letting him go. She's visionary in that she perhaps sees what he will become more clearly than he can. I think in another time and another place she was a warrior as well. She's a support for these women around her and all that they are truly capable of being. She loves unconditionally. [*Bassett gets called to leave early for work on FOX's* 9-1-1 *series and departs the group.*] I love you. Kisses all around!

In Shuri's case, you can tell T'Challa really respects his little sister because he takes so much abuse and mockery from her.

[*Laughter all around*]

LW She's a relatable character to other young girls, with that brother-sister vibe. He respects not only Shuri but all the women. He holds his own as a man and a king, but he respects everyone and what they're doing.

What surprised you about Shuri as you found the character?

LW When I read the comic books, she's serious all the time. With the script, they wanted her to be smart, but she is so much fun. She picks on her brother, and she makes jokes.... [*Laughs*] Always got something fiery to say.

LN What I love about Nakia is she's worldly. She speaks many languages. And she's a chameleon in a sense. She is at once extremely rebellious and wants to do her own thing but wants to do well by her country. I love that tension in her. I love her relationship with T'Challa. It's ...complicated. [*Laughs*] That's the Facebook status.

It humanizes him. It takes the—

LN —the edge off. He's just a guy. I love the distinction between Okoye and Nakia, who insists she's not a member of the Dora Milaje.

DG She didn't go through the process, the training!

That unifying power seems special to Okoye, like that's one of her strengths.

DG I envision her as a very intense young girl who was competitive but in a good way. She's part of the border tribe and very connected to the idea of nation protection. She's a protector. I imagine her as a very focused 12-year-old. [*Laughs*] There was this idea I had whenever Okoye or any of the army are in the streets, that little girls look up to them and want to wear that uniform one day. She was once that little girl. She is a very strong traditionalist. She believes in holding the country together.

When you were shooting this, *Wonder Woman* hadn't come out, and some questioned if women would turn out for a superhero movie. Do you feel a change in the way audiences want female heroes?

DG I never doubted that. People decide

things based on lack. You don't provide, and then you say people don't want things. But they didn't have options on the table, so how can you really make that assessment? I actually think it's the opposite. It was then learned through *Wonder Woman,* which was no surprise to most women. We were all ready to flock out to that.

***Black Panther* is also hitting right in the heart of the #MeToo and #TimesUp movement. Does it draw energy from that with its many powerful women characters?**

LN I feel very strongly that change is not an event, it's a process. What we see happening in this moment is pivotal. It's not over. We cannot assess it yet. We have to keep going.

DUKE OF WAKANDA

It's okay to laugh with Winston Duke, the actor behind M'Baku in Black Panther. **BY ANTHONY BREZNICAN**

***Black Panther* has a secret** weapon—M'Baku, the charismatic leader of the separatist Jabari mountain tribe, who thinks he'd do a better job leading Wakanda than young King T'Challa (Chadwick Boseman). In Marvel Comics lore, M'Baku was an unabashed threat. In the film, actor Winston Duke makes him a triple threat: dangerous, sure, but also charming and—surprisingly—noble.

The move to make M'Baku more grounded was intentional, says Duke, 31, who until now was best known for the CBS drama *Person of Interest.* "He's faced with the same question T'Challa is: By staying isolated, what world are we gonna create outside of ourselves?"

M'Baku is also hilarious "because he knows how he is perceived," says the 6'5" actor, who plays that fearsomeness for laughs. "We got to explore this guy who everyone thought was going to be something else, and we turned it on its head."

Duke recalls seeing *The Avengers* with his Yale School of Drama colleague (and *Black Panther* costar) Lupita Nyong'o in 2012. "We were both enamored with the Hulk. We were all like, 'Aaargh!' every time Hulk got on the screen," he says. "And we had moments of 'Do you think we'll ever be in something like this?' That was before *12 Years a Slave.* Before anything. We were both just students dreaming, 'What's the future going to be like?'"

The future, for both, turned out to be Wakanda. But it is certainly not their last stop.

TRIBAL WAVE

Wakanda may be fictional, but its style is rooted in real history. Not only did costumer Ruth E. Carter need to outfit individual characters—including the Black Panther himself, T'Challa (Chadwick Boseman)—she also had to establish a cohesive look for an entire country, one that's both futuristic and steeped in ancient African tradition. **BY DEVAN COGGAN**

1

PURPLE REIGN
The shaman Zuri (Forest Whitaker) is a mentor for T'Challa, and to give him that sense of reverence, Carter based his look on ancient Nigerian chiefs, adding intricate pleating inspired by Japanese fashion designer Issey Miyake.

2

FIT FOR A QUEEN
As Wakanda's queen mother, Ramonda (Angela Bassett) looks appropriately regal. The shoulder mantle is inspired by Victorian ruffs, and her 3-D-printed headpiece mimics traditional Zulu hats. "I felt that there would be people who would make beautiful pieces for her, and they would be the most forward-thinking pieces in the whole universe," Carter says.

3

CASINO ROYALE
Nakia (Lupita Nyong'o) wears this glam green dress to infiltrate a casino with T'Challa. The textured fabric is similar to African kente cloth; should trouble arise, it's also stretchy and practical for fighting.

4

PUT A RING ON IT
Okoye (Danai Gurira) leads the Dora Milaje, Wakanda's elite female fighting force. Carter kept the deep red color from the comics but added Vibranium necklaces and cuffs, modeled on the neck rings worn by Ndebele women. "The neck rings needed to have a hand-done feel," Carter says. "Most jewelry you see from Africa looks like someone hammered it and molded it by hand."

5

IT STAYS IN THE FAMILY
The Dora Milaje also wear elaborately beaded tabards and harnesses. "I imagine that these Dora Milaje train their daughters, and when she's ready to join the force, the mother who's retiring could take off her harness and hand it down," Carter says.

4
5
ANTHONY FRANCISCO
2016

ENTERTAINMENT WEEKLY
Editorial Director Jess Cagle
Editor Henry Goldblatt
Executive Editor Tim Leong

AVENGERS: INFINITY WAR
Editor Alyssa Smith
Editor, People + EW Books Allison Adato
Executive Editor Gina McIntyre
Art Director Sung Choi
Photo Editor Robert Conway
Photo Editor, People + EW Books C. Tiffany Lee-Ramos
Writers Anthony Breznican, Sean Smith, Chancellor Agard, Devan Coggan, Clark Collis, Glenn Greenberg, Jeff Labrecque, John Jackson Miller, Piya Sinha-Roy
Reporter Daniel S. Levy
Copy Desk Joanann Scali (Chief), James Bradley (Deputy), Ellen Adamson, Gabrielle Danchick, Richard Donnelly, Ben Harte, Rose Kaplan, Matt Weingarden (Copy Editors)
Production Designer Peter Niceberg
Premedia Executive Director Richard Prue
Senior Manager Romeo Cifelli
Manager Rob Roszkowski
Imaging Production Associates Franklin Abreu, Ana Kaljaj
Research Director Céline Wojtala

TIME INC. BOOKS
A DIVISION OF MEREDITH CORPORATION
Publisher Margot Schupf
Senior Vice President, Finance Anthony Palumbo
Vice President, Marketing Jeremy Biloon
Executive Director, Marketing Services Carol Pittard
Director, Brand Marketing Jean Kennedy
Sales Director Christi Crowley
Associate Director, Brand Marketing Bryan Christian
Associate Director, Finance Jill Earyes
Assistant General Counsel Andrew Goldberg
Senior Manager, Finance Ashley Petrasovic
Senior Brand Manager Katherine Barnet
Prepress Manager Alex Voznesenskiy
Associate Project and Production Manager Anna Riego Muñiz

Editorial Director Kostya Kennedy
Creative Director Gary Stewart
Director of Photography Christina Lieberman
Editorial Operations Director Jamie Roth Major
Manager, Editorial Operations Gina Scauzillo

SPECIAL THANKS
Brad Beatson, Brett Finkelstein, Melissa Frankenberry, Kristina Jutzi, Simon Keeble, Seniqua Koger, Kate Roncinske

Published by Time Inc. Books,
A division of Meredith Corporation
225 Liberty Street
New York, NY 10281

We welcome your comments and suggestions about Entertainment Weekly Books. Please write to us at: Entertainment Weekly Books, Attention: Book Editors, P.O. Box 62310, Tampa, FL 33662-2310
If you would like to order any of our hardcover Collector's Edition books, please call us at 800-327-6388, Monday through Friday, 7 a.m.–9 p.m. Central Time.

PHOTO CREDITS
COVER: ©Marvel Studios 2018; **BACK COVER:** (top) ©Marvel Studios; Chuck Zlotnick/©Marvel Studios; **Pg 1:** Marco Grob/©Marvel Studios; **Pg 2:** ©Marvel Studios; **Pg 4:** Iron Man: The Embassy; ©Marvel Studios(2); **Pg 6:** ©Marvel Studios; **Pg 8-9:** ©Marvel Studios(2); **Pg 10-11:** ©Marvel Studios(2); **Pg 12-13:** (top) ©Marvel Studios, Chuck Zlotnick/©Marvel Studios; **Pg 14-15:** ©Marvel Studios; **Pg 16-17:** Koury Angelo; **Pg 18-19:** Justin Fantl; **Pg 20-21:** Zade Rosenthal/©Marvel Studios; **Pg 22-23:** Zade Rosenthal/©Marvel Studios; **Pg 24-25:** ©Marvel Studios; **Pg 26-27:** 1, 4: Zade Rosenthal/©Marvel

Front Row (L to R): Sean Gunn, Hannah John-Kamen, Scott Derrickson, Trinh Tran, Jeremy Renner, Paul Rudd, Victoria Alonso, Zoe Saldana, Angela Bassett, Jon Favreau, Chris Hemsworth, Gwyneth Paltrow, Chris Evans, Robert Downey Jr., Stan Lee, Kevin Feige, Scarlett Johansson, Louis D'Esposito, Kurt Russell, Danai Gurira, William Hurt, Alan Taylor, Karen Gillan, Brad Winderbaum, Emily VanCamp, Louis Letterier. **Second Row:** Jon Watts, Sarah Finn, Tessa Thompson, David Grant, Don Cheadle, Tom Holland, James Gunn, Dave Bautista, Michael Peña, Anthony Mackie, Evangeline Lilly, Joe Russo, Anthony Russo, Chris Pratt, Chadwick Boseman, Benedict Cumberbatch, Elizabeth Olsen, Joss Whedon, Paul Bettany, Mitchell Bell, Frank Grillo, Anna Boden, Ryan Fleck, Letitia Wright, Jeffrey Ford. **Third Row:** Peyton Reed, Laurence Fishburne, Linda Cardellini, Jonathan Schwartz, Sebastian Stan, Ty Simpkins, Mark Ruffalo, Brie Larson, Michael Douglas, Stephen Broussard, Ryan Coogler, Michelle Pfeiffer, Jeremy Latcham, Hayley Atwell, Pom Klementieff, Nate Moore, Benedict Wong. **Fourth Row:** Christopher Markus, Stephen McFeely, Michael Rooker, Vin Diesel, Cobie Smulders, Samuel L. Jackson, Taika Waititi, Jeff Goldblum, Eric Carroll, Ryan Meinerding, Craig Kyle.

Studios(2); 2, 3: ©Marvel Studios(2); **Pg 28-29:** 6, 8, 10: ©Marvel Studios(3); 7: Matt Kennedy/©Marvel Studios; 8: Zade Rosenthal/©Marvel Studios; **Pg 30-31:** ©Marvel Studios(5); War Machine: Industrial Light & Magic/ ©Marvel Studios; shield: Justin Fantl; Winter, Scarlet: Zade Rosenthal/©Marvel Studios(2); Widow: Francois Duhamel/Paramount; Ant: Ben Rothstein/©Marvel Studios; **Pg 32-33:** ©Marvel Studios; **Pg 35:** Koury Angelo; **Pg 36:** Michael Muller/©Marvel Studios; **Pg 37:** Iron Man 2: Francois Duhamel/©Marvel Studios; Iron Man 3: Zade Rosenthal/©Marvel Studios; **Pg 38-39:** ©Marvel Studios; **Pg 40:** ©Marvel Studios; **Pg 41:** Hawkeye: Jay Maidment/©Marvel Studios; War Machine: Industrial Light & Magic/©Marvel Studios; **Pg 42-43:** ©Marvel Studios; **Pg 45:** Matthias Clamer; **Pg 46-47:** Zade Rosenthal/©Marvel Studios; **Pg 48-49:** Robert Gauthier/Los Angeles Times/Contour by Getty Images; **Pg 50-51:** Captain America: ©Marvel Studios; Black Widow: Marco Grob/©Marvel Studios; **Pg 52-53:** Justin Fantl; **Pg 54-55:** ©Marvel Studios(2); Scarlet: Zade Rosenthal/ ©Marvel Studios; **Pg 56-57:** Rudd: ©Marvel Studios; Ant Man and the Wasp: Ben Rothstein/©Marvel Studios; Rudd and Lily: Zade Rosenthal/©Marvel Studios; **Pg 58-59:** ©Marvel Studios(7); Thor: Mark Fellman/ ©Marvel Studios; Loki, Drax: Chuck Zlotnick/©Marvel Studios(2); Heimdall: Jasin Boland/©Marvel Studios; Strange: Jay Maidment/©Marvel Studios; **Pg 60-61:** ©Marvel Studios; **Pg 63:** Koury Angelo; **Pg 64-65:** Justin Fantl; **Pg 66-67:** Loki: ©Marvel Studios; Heimdall: Jasin Boland/©Marvel Studios; **Pg 68-69:** ©Marvel Studios(2); **Pg 70-71:** ©Marvel Studios; **Pg 72-73:** lineup: ©Marvel Studios; Nebula: Chuck Zlotnick/ ©Marvel Studios; **Pg 74-75:** Strange: Jay Maidment/ ©Marvel Studios; Cumberbatch: Koury Angelo; Eye: Justin Fantl; **Pg 76-77:** Black Panther: Ryan Meinderding/ ©Marvel Studios; Matt Kennedy/©Marvel Studios(5); **Pg 78-79:** ©Marvel Studios; **Pg 80-81:** Koury Angelo: **Pg 82-83:** ©Marvel Studios; **Pg 84-85:** Kenya: Yasuyoshi Chiba/AFP/Getty Images; Coates, Boseman, Nyong'o: Shahar Azran/WireImage; **Pg 86-87:** Koury Angelo; **Pg 88-89:** ©Marvel Studios; **Pg 90-91:** Queen: Matt Kennedy/©Marvel Studios; Duke: Kwaku Alston/ ©Marvel Studios; **Pg 92:** Zuri: Ruth Carter & Phillip Boutte Jr./©Marvel Studios; Ramonda: Ruth Carter, Ryan Meinerding & Team/©Marvel Studios; Nakia: Ruth Carter & Keith Christensen/©Marvel Studios; **Pg 93:** Dora Milaje: Ryan Meinderding, VisDev Team, & Anthony Franciso/©Marvel Studios; **Pg 94-95:** Marco Grob/ ©Marvel Studios; **Pg 96:** Marco Grob/ ©Marvel Studios

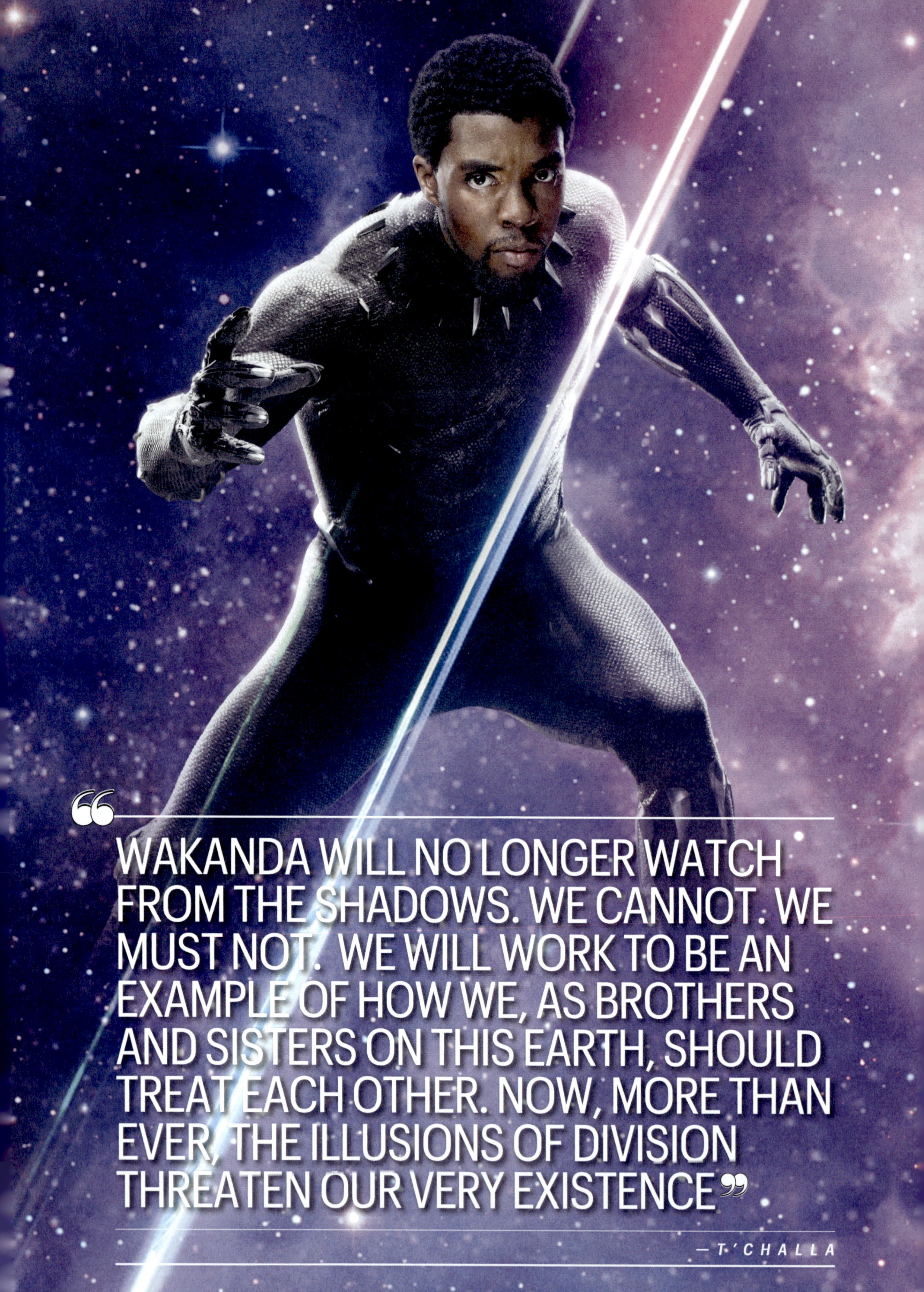
“WAKANDA WILL NO LONGER WATCH FROM THE SHADOWS. WE CANNOT. WE MUST NOT. WE WILL WORK TO BE AN EXAMPLE OF HOW WE, AS BROTHERS AND SISTERS ON THIS EARTH, SHOULD TREAT EACH OTHER. NOW, MORE THAN EVER, THE ILLUSIONS OF DIVISION THREATEN OUR VERY EXISTENCE”
—T'CHALLA

Made in the USA
Middletown, DE
02 May 2019